BRU...

But Not Broken

The Journey from Heartache to Healing

Sheryl Beck-Nelson
© 2014

Creative Force Press

Creative Force Press

Bruised but Not Broken
© 2014 by Sheryl Beck-Nelson
www.sherylbecknelson.com

This title is also available as an eBook. Visit
www.CreativeForcePress.com/titles for more information.

Published by Creative Force Press
4704 Pacific Ave, Suite C, Lacey, WA 98503
www.CreativeForcePress.com

ISBN: 978-1-939989-15-4

Printed in the United States of America
Cover design by www.IRCprintanddesign.com

Dedicated to
Mathew Taylor Beck
The Unbreakable Boy

Table of Contents

Chapter 1:

Love and Loss

"Mostly it is loss which teaches us about the worth of things."
–Arthur Schopenhauer

My best stories start out with "When I was a little girl…" Well, when I was a little girl growing up in church, there was a song that was very popular (I'm gonna date myself here, but I'm fine with that). The song is called *Give Them All to Jesus*, and the chorus says, "Give them all, give them all, give them all to Jesus, shattered dreams, wounded hearts and broken toys. Give them all, give them all, give them all to Jesus and He will turn your sorrow into joy." It has a catchy tune and when you're young, that's really all that matters, right? However, as a grown woman, the tune is still quite catchy, but I have found my life in the lyrics of this song. You see, awhile back my life was shaken up. Let me tell you the story…

February 26, 2012. It was a Sunday and my 11 year old son Mathew and I were home that day. Our church had multiple services each weekend, and it just so happened that my husband, Rich, was playing electric guitar on the worship team that weekend. Mathew and I had gone to the Saturday evening service, so we spent Sunday at home chillin' together. Our close family friends, the Creek family, were coming over that night to watch the Oscars, so it was a day we had really been looking forward to.

All was normal. Rich got home from church and I started working on our *red carpet* snacks for the evening. Surviving the Oscars requires sustenance. It's a long night. If you've ever watched them, you know what I'm talking about!

Our life was fairly low key, and this evening was no different. Our two families split up into two groups: the couch set of "Good Lord, that dress is hideous, oh wait...is that Colin Firth?!" and the dining room set of "Let me show you this new guitar riff I have been working on." This was all very normal for us.

As the evening wore on, the food disappeared, the Oscars ended and the small Creeks, Nyah and Aislynne, got sleepy. We exchanged hugs and "massive kisses" and they went home. It was late, so we headed to bed. Not too long after going to bed, Rich got up complaining of pressure in his chest. This was *not* normal. He asked me to call 911 and I went into immediate freak-out mode. He wasn't a *call 911* kinda guy, so I was scared.

After the paramedics came and checked him out, they decided he should go to the hospital and took him away in the ambulance. I woke Mathew and we followed close behind; so close in fact that I could see every time the paramedic in the back of the ambulance moved. It was the longest 20-minute drive in the history of driving.

When we finally finished the hospital check–in process, it was a lot of hurry up and wait. The tests they had to perform had to be monitored hourly, and we basically waited for them to rule out different scenarios. After about 5 hours, the doctors realized the problem; an aortic rupture. In laymen's and freaked out wives' terms, that means a rip in his heart. After that, things started moving with lightning speed.

The doctors knew the problem and were eager to fix it. They were clear with me the seriousness of the situation. The only option was a long surgery — 12 hours — in which they would stop his heart, put him on bypass, repair the rupture, and start his heart again. Spoken as a to-do list, it all seemed completely manageable, but they explained to me that it was *anything but*.

The doctors and nurses prepared Rich for surgery, and right before they were ready to wheel him out of his room, he hugged and kissed Mathew and told him he loved him. Next, he kissed me, gave me his wedding ring and said, "Don't worry. It'll be fine." He also asked me to alert our friends through social media so they could be agreeing with us in prayer. We rode the huge elevator together and then said one more *I love you* as they wheeled him into the operating room to be prepped for surgery.

I called our friend Matt, who had been our pastor before we moved, and asked him to come be with us. I knew he would be a rock in a difficult situation, and I needed that support. He arrived just before the surgeon came out to tell us they were ready to begin. The surgeon assured me a nurse would be calling me every hour to keep us updated on Rich's progress. Matt prayed over the surgeon and his team, then he went back in to give the Lord and Rich his best.

We called family and close friends telling them the situation and asked for prayer. Rich's family all lived in California, so I called Rich's brother to let him know what was happening. It is then that I discovered that Rich's dad had recently come out strong from the exact same surgery, and so his family wasn't worried that the outcome would be anything but favorable.

As believers, we go into situations with a *God has this covered* attitude, blanketed in faith and trust, knowing that there is nothing outside the realm of the Lord's control. As a daughter of the Almighty, I believe this wholeheartedly. As an exhausted wife on the other hand, I was scared to death!

By this time it was morning. Mathew and I had been up all night, so we were sleep deprived. A friend came to get Mathew so he could go back to Matt's house and sleep. We were selective about whom to have at the hospital with us, ending up with a small group that consisted of both friends and family. They encouraged me to sleep, but when it became obvious that wasn't going to happen, they kept me distracted between the nurse's update phone calls.

For many hours, his calls were consistently relaying *everything is going as planned*, until all of a sudden they weren't. When they took him off bypass, his heart wouldn't beat on its own, so they had to put him back on bypass. The nurse was very upfront with me about the fact that this was not a good situation. It was at that point that I started to melt down a little; mind, body and emotions all stretched to the breaking point.

I found myself curled up on the bathroom floor, completely spent. My best friend, Jen, was there with me on the floor, and she said this, "No matter what happens, he's going to be okay." I knew what she meant; that he would be healed, or he would be in Heaven, but I'm telling you right now, I wanted to punch her in the face. I didn't...she totally dodged that bullet, but I really wanted to! I told her to stop talking. I didn't want truth in that moment; it was both painful and beautiful, but I couldn't see the beauty. I could only feel the stabs to my heart that pulsed *you may lose him.*

Finally, after several more hours, the surgery was over. The surgeon, the same man that we had prayed for so many hours ago, came to me exhausted and spent. It had been an ordeal for him, as well as for the rest of us. He told us that Rich's heart was pumping on its own, but his blood wouldn't clot. He was on a constant blood transfusion, but there was nothing else they could do.

By then, my friend, Crystal (Matt's wife), had arrived. I turned to my friend, the walking concordance, and said, "I need Heaven verses. He's going there, and I need to hear how wonderful it is!" She came through! "Eye has not seen... Ear has not heard..." It calmed me. I was able to refocus on Jesus and told Him that no matter what happened, it was me and HIM, I loved HIM no matter the outcome of my family's situation.

For the next 17 hours, we took turns holding Rich's hand, talking to him, and praying in his room. We worshipped, singing songs he loved; songs like *Mighty to Save* and *Beautiful Exchange*. I was able to get some sleep and felt a bit refreshed. With my faith in the Lord renewed, I prayed a fervent prayer of faith with our group in the waiting room. Knowing who my Jesus was, I believed for healing.

Rich held on...longer than doctors expected, but still wasn't improving. I started to consider the possibility that the outcome I desired and the outcome the Lord had ordained were not the same. So, I told Rich, "Come alongside whatever the Lord is doing. If He's going to heal you then you better hold on, but if He's not, it's okay."

And so, on February 28th 2012 at 11:15 AM, with our friend Matt at his side, my husband and friend went to be with Jesus...to play amazing worship music for his King. He attained the goal for which we are all striving. I was jealous; jealous of Rich that he got to be with Jesus, and jealous of Jesus that He got to be with Rich. I had been so sure that Rich would be healed at the brink of death and would have an amazing testimony. Instead, the testimony is mine.

It was completely devastating. Though my faith was firmly placed upon my infinitely powerful and unmoving God, I was crushed. I called Jen, who, with her husband Dane, had gone home for a little while to check on their daughters. When I reached her, they were in the car on the way back to hospital. When she answered the phone all I said was, "You don't need to come." Her voice cracked as she said, "But we're on our way," Even though she knew all along it would end this way, (something I didn't know until later) she was still heartbroken. Her pain was not just for me, her best friend who had lost a spouse, but also for her spouse, Dane, who had lost a best friend.

My friend, Beth, called to check on me almost immediately after I got off the phone with Jen. She had been keeping our worship team updated with Rich's progress, and like me, she had fully expected the Lord to perform a miraculous healing. The conversation with her, the pain in her voice, helped me to understand how significant Rich was to our worship team. In that moment, I realized I couldn't be selfish in my grief. The loss was not just mine and Mathew's, it belonged to everyone who loved Rich.

The drive home from the hospital was a lot different than you might expect. It was different than what I expected anyway. I anticipated feeling heavy, weighed down by the events of the day, but I didn't. Don't get me wrong, I was devastated and realistically probably still in shock, but what I felt…*who* I felt, was Jesus. When we got in the car Crystal immediately turned on a worship CD. It was perfect. We sang to the Lord; worship pulled from the deepest parts of our spirits. It was the most intimate time of worship I have ever experienced, and I was so grateful for that time with Him. It equipped me for the difficult conversation I was about to have with our son, Mathew.

When we pulled up to Matt and Crystal's house, where Mathew was resting, we just sat in the car for a moment. Matt said, "Sheryl, I know this is going to be hard, but you can't cry when you talk to Mathew. You have be strong for him." The idea of saying the words "Your dad *died*," dry-eyed seemed impossible, so we prayed. Matt prayed that the Holy Spirit would direct every word and help me to be whatever Mathew needed.

When I felt ready, we headed into the house. When I sat down next to him, he looked at me and asked, "Is he dead?" It seemed abrupt, but I knew he was purposefully asking in a way that seemed ridiculous, hoping I would say, "Of course not!" Unfortunately, I had to answer, "Yes," and then held him while he cried. I told him how much his dad loved him, which was immense, and assured him that his dad would never have left him on purpose. We sat there together for a long time, our pain severe, holding on tightly to one another; the remnants of a family that was broken.

I also began to feel as though I needed to acknowledge the impact Rich's death was having on the worship team and to thank them for their love and prayers. They are family to us, and I needed to reach out to them. Our team is large, so I decided the best way for me to do this was through our team's Facebook page. I thought long and hard about what to say, and finally sat to write this painful message:

So I told Rich this morning that it was gonna be a great day and that whatever the Lord was doing, he should come alongside Him. No matter the outcome, God was and is in control. It has turned out to be the most marvelous day for Rich. Today he is with Jesus, playing crazy guitar riffs at Jesus' feet. Loving his new home and shouting "Yeeaahhh!" as he rounds every corner. He is feeling awesome and I am truly happy for him and blessed to have a husband that I know without a doubt is in Heaven. Mathew and I are of course struggling with the outcome of the day, but we have an amazing support system surrounding us, and we trust in the Lord and KNOW that all things work for good. I know you are all praying and have been since the beginning, and I can't tell you how much I appreciate it. Please continue to pray for me and Mathew, as nothing feels quite real and we're in a haze. Let me encourage you all, as I know you have lost a friend; to be absent from the body is to be present with the Lord and really, isn't that what we're all aiming for? Rich just got there before us...show off! We love you guys and thank you for everything!" We were all in this together, and so we'll all heal together; me, Mathew, our friends, and our church family.

Chapter 2:

The Memorial

"Grief is the price we pay for love." –Queen Elizabeth II

The next few days were overwhelming, but I had people around who loved me. They knew me well enough to know how to help without me really needing to ask. Mathew and I decided to move out of our house and move in with our friends, Matt and Crystal, and their kids, Gabe and Faith. Strangely, it was a seamless transition. I have always lived like our friends were family, which made the move feel very comfortable.

My friends helped spearhead the move out of the house, and moving day couldn't get there fast enough. It was extremely difficult, physically and emotionally, but was made much easier by all the help. Many of Rich's co-workers from State Farm, people I had never even met before, came to do whatever they could to make the day more bearable for me. They took time to help a woman they didn't know because they had admired her husband. I think it speaks to the kind of person Rich was, and I appreciated each of them.

Once we were moved out and settled in our new home, all that was left was the memorial. Rich had been in the Air Force, and was to be buried at Tahoma National Cemetery in Maple Valley, Washington. My friend, Shelly, took care of the details for me, and I can't tell you how much it meant to be able to trust someone else with those details. Her brain works perfectly in that capacity and I'm so grateful! Both the ceremony at the National Cemetery and a more personal memorial service were scheduled for March 8, 2012.

Anticipating a deeply painful service, I was very selective about who was invited to the burial, wanting to share that moment with only those whom I felt completely safe; people that had meant something to Rich and our family in a genuine way. Mathew was front row, center, and cried the entire time. I held his hand on my left and Jen's hand on my right. The gunfire was deafening and full of the sound of finality. At the very end of the service, an Air Force NCOIC knelt in front of Mathew and said, "On behalf of the President of the United States, the Air Force and a grateful nation, I am sorry for the loss of your loved one," while handing him his dad's flag that had just been perfectly folded in front of us. It was a crushing two hours, and I felt completely numb. We left for home, to rest, have something to eat and prepare for the memorial. It was to be the party that Rich deserved.

The Bible says to rejoice when we lose someone to Heaven. It was an enormous loss for us, but an unimaginable gain for Rich, and we intended to celebrate both of them; who Rich was with us and who Jesus is to all of us. Nearly 300 people who loved and admired my husband celebrated with us that afternoon; celebrating the husband, father, friend and worshipper that he was.

I know funerals often feel dark and heavy, but his memorial didn't. The church was bright from the late afternoon sunlight pouring in through the tall windows. People were chatting and hugging, no doubt sharing stories about the friend they had lost. I had been curious, bordering on nervous about the size of the room and whether or not it would be overwhelming. Would I feel exposed and vulnerable? However, once the service started, it didn't occur to me to think about any of those things anymore. I realized that vulnerability wasn't something I needed to be afraid of. I just needed to experience each aspect of the day as it happened. I allowed myself to feel whatever I was feeling and let the Lord use it as He saw fit.

We started with worship. I chose songs that had meaning: *Beautiful Exchange*, which had been his favorite worship song, and *Mighty to Save*, which we had sung to him in the hospital room. During this song, 18 guitarists played along with the worship team. It was amazing. They lined the aisles, and I can say with confidence it was Rich's favorite part of the day. From the front row I could see every one of them, sad, but honored to play one last time for their friend. Lastly, *Rooftops*, the song we sang on the way home from the hospital was played. It had become my anthem. When you feel lost, there is so much power in singing the words, "So I shout out your name, from the rooftops I proclaim, that I am Yours."

Matt gave the eulogy in perfect "Matt Fashion," being both funny and heart-warming. He talked about his friend with love, all the while joking about who we all knew him to be. He spoke about Rich being one of the few men who would not only make his peace with his wife putting a Christmas tree up in early November, but would actually defend her if someone dared mention that this was somehow odd. He told stories of Rich's love for science and desire to discuss the amazing achievements of Nikola Tesla despite the fact that very few of us even knew who Nikola Tesla was, much less understood the profound achievement of the Tesla coil. He reiterated to the crowd that Rich was deeply committed to using his musical ability to honor God and found a reason to practice at pretty much every get together we ever had. Not that we needed reminding, but his words reminded us of the quirkiness that made Rich who he was.

It was wonderful. I know it's weird to describe a eulogy as *wonderful*, but the truth is, the entire memorial was *wonderful*. I remember laughing as Matt shared with the crowd what a great match Rich and I were; the calm, steady husband and the slightly wacky wife. As cliché as it may sound, we laughed, we cried and we laughed again. Several people, including Rich's youngest brother stood up to express a quick thought or story. They shared with the crowd how Rich had impacted them in life and in ministry. The Lord was clearly present in that place. There was tangible proof of the scripture found in Psalms 34:18a (MSG): "If your heart is broken, you'll find GOD right there."

All in all, it was as perfect as a memorial can be. I felt the strength of the people around me and the love they had for me and Mathew. It was exhausting, but there can be joy in the memorial of one who we have lost to Heaven.

Chapter 3:

The Reboot

"The last page turned is a perfect excuse to write a whole new book." –Toni Sorenson

Finally, with nothing left to plan, it was time to focus on what our new lives would look like. We tried to get back in the swing of things as best we could. Mathew started back to school, and we both got into the routine of living with the Krachunis family. They are the pastors of a non-denominational church in Auburn, Washington. It was the church we had actually attended and served in prior to our present church. Mathew and I split our time between Matt and Crystal's church in Auburn and our church in Lacey.

I returned to the worship team for the Easter weekend services. It had been about 6 weeks since Rich died, and though I knew it may be a struggle, I desperately wanted to be back and doing what I love; something for which I was created. It was a rough rehearsal for me. We sang Beautiful Exchange, which we had just done for Rich's memorial, and though I knew it was on the schedule, I still felt caught off guard. I melted down in front of the team. The prideful part of me was so annoyed and embarrassed, but deep down I knew I was safe to be vulnerable with these people. There was no judgment, only pain as they hurt for me. When there is nothing that you can actually do for a person, the best thing is to just stand with them, and that's what the worship team did for me.

My wonderful friend Evan stood next to me, angling his body so I wouldn't be as visible to the rest of the team. I will forever remember that moment and how he tried to stand guard over my weakened emotional state.

Worship born out of pain, can be the most beautiful, and that's what I experienced that weekend. It was a celebration of my risen Savior, and through that Easter weekend, I began to feel the strength of my God rising up in me.

It was around that time that Rich's grave stone was to be ready at the National Cemetery. I wanted to go see it by myself before I took Mathew. So, I prepared myself mentally and emotionally for the vast grandness that is Tahoma National Cemetery. I also prepared for the intimate moment that I was about to experience with Jesus, and Rich who was with Him.

I pulled up to the grassy landscape where my husband's ashes were buried and just sat in the car for a few minutes with the Lord. When I was finally ready, I got out of the car. It was spring in the Northwest and very wet out. I walked around on the outer parts of the grass, because I didn't want to walk in the space between the gravestones; it seemed somehow disrespectful. I had only taken a few steps before I had completely sunk into the mud. I was in deep; so deep in fact, that I couldn't see my feet anymore. My feet were swallowed up and the cuffs of my pants were covered in mud.

I was annoyed. My conversation, well, more accurately, my monologue with the Lord went something like this. "Seriously Lord?! You know I'm already struggling with this. This is already not a good time, and now I'm stuck in mud? This is ridiculous and not at all okay with me!" I was saying it out loud and with a little bit of attitude.

When I tried to free my feet from the mud, my feet came, but my shoes didn't. I had to reach in pull them out of the mud and carry them with me to see Rich's grave stone. When I got there, it was with mixed emotions; sadness for myself and Mathew, excitement for Rich, and annoyance at God about the mud.

Rich wasn't stuck in the mud – he was having a great day in Heaven. The Bible only tells us a sliver of the beauty of Heaven, but it was now his new normal, if you can call Heaven *normal*. I was upset with God about the mud. I felt it had taken away some of my dignity in a moment when, from my standpoint, dignity was all I had. My thought process was already pretty messy, and seeing Rich's name on a stone in the ground added to the bizarre mess. Looking at it was like a slap in the face that said, "This is for real and you need to make your peace with it."

I hadn't made my peace with it. My eyes were fixated on the date of his final day: February 28, 2012. It took me back to the hospital and every emotion that encompassed me there. I had, at moments, rested in a cocoon of hope, only to have to let it fall away from my soul and accept the finality. Rich was actually gone. Gone!? How could that be? How could this have happened? I'm sure the Lord hears that question a lot from visitors of cemeteries.

I believe that the Lord saw me standing there, sad and alone. He knew I needed Rich's attention, so I believe God called to him: "Rich, come on over here. Your girl wants to talk to you for a bit." Confident he was paying attention, I started with small talk. After all, it felt awkward to talk in this manner to the man with whom I had shared my life. I told him I liked where his plot was and that he would think it was wonderful and peaceful. I described the trees and the many beautiful shades of green he was surrounded by. He had always loved living in Washington, full of beautiful trees everywhere.

As I grew more comfortable with talking to him, I shared about how Mathew was doing. "Mathew really misses you, but he is doing really well despite everything." I assured him I *would* bring Mathew to visit the site, but this first time I needed him all to myself. I promised I would take really great care of his boy, and that I saw the husband I lost in the face of his son every day.

I told him that I always assumed I would die first, so living without him was something for which I felt unprepared. I tried to convey to him the confidence that I had in the Lord, and laughed a little knowing that he was actually with God as I spoke of Him.

After some time, I headed back to my car. My awareness that I was walking in bare feet gave me a welcome reprieve from my painful emotions. That day, I had processed them as far as I could, so I allowed my thoughts to shift to something more manageable.

As I got in my car, I thought to myself, "Stuck in the mud?!?!? How embarrassing! I'm never going to tell anyone that this happened." That resolve lasted about 8 minutes, until I got on the phone with my friend, Trish, telling her the whole absurd story. She had the good sense to wait until we hung up to laugh out loud about it.

As frustrating as this scenario felt in the moment, it was a clear turning point for me. The Lord was speaking to me through this experience. "Sheryl, yes, it is ridiculous for you to be stuck in the mud feeling trapped. I'm glad you're annoyed by it. See how even more ridiculous it would be for you to stay stuck in the mire of your feelings of loss and stagnation. I don't want you trapped by what you are feeling. I have plans for you and you cannot accomplish them if you're stuck. I want so much more for you!"

I turned a corner that day and I began to feel like myself again. Praise God! The life I would be experiencing from that day forward was not what I had expected or planned for, but it was the life the Lord had ordained for me. He had confidence that I would thrive and grow through it all, which encouraged confidence in me that He would walk beside me, working His will through it all.

Chapter 4:

A New Thing

God's speaking... are you listening?

Looking back, I realized that He had been giving me a subtle heads up that something was going to be different: a new season was ahead. Two months before Rich died, I started having dreams I was pregnant. While I thought it was interesting and kind of funny, I didn't put any stock in the first pregnancy dream. We did not plan on having any more children. However, the dreams became so consistent, I began wondering what the scenario of my pregnancy would be the next time. The truth is, the Lord was trying to tell me something; He was preparing me for something new. Like a painful, strenuous pregnancy and labor, my new season would be painful and full of difficulty that I would need to push through. But, at the end I would see the amazing hand of God bringing about His will, working all things for my good. Romans 8:28, (NKJ) translation says, "And we know that all things work together for good to those who love God, to those who are called according to His purpose."

Interestingly, in The Message translation, Romans 8:26-28 says, "Meanwhile, the moment we get tired in the waiting, God's Spirit is right alongside helping us along. If we don't know how or what to pray, it doesn't matter. He does our praying in and for us, making prayer out of our wordless sighs, our aching groans. He knows us far better than we know ourselves, knows **our pregnant condition**, and keeps us present before God. That's why we can be so sure that every detail in our lives of love for God is worked into something good."

He not only knows our pregnant condition, but is alongside us through the labor required to bring about the new thing. Isaiah 43:19 says "Behold, **I will do a new thing**, now it shall spring forth; shall you not know it? I will even make a road in the wilderness and rivers in the desert." It was to these scriptures I held firm.

I also found immense comfort in the words of many worship songs. Certain songs I had been singing on the worship team spoke so perfectly to my situation. "One thing remains…Your love never fails, never gives up, never runs out on me!" I also had friends who brought songs to my attention; songs that captured the heart of my life in those moments. "I know that You are for me, I know that You are for me, I know that You will never forsake me in my weaknesses."

A New Song

There was another song that proved so helpful in my healing process. It was a song I had written a short time before Rich had died. It was originally written about the woman with the issue of blood (Luke 8:43-48), who pushed through the masses to touch the hem of Jesus' garment. "Now a woman, having a flow of blood for twelve years, who had spent all her livelihood on physicians and could not be healed by any, came from behind and touched the border of His garment. And immediately her flow of blood stopped. And Jesus said, 'Who touched Me?' When all denied it, Peter and those with him said, 'Master, the multitudes throng and press You, and You say, 'Who touched Me?' But Jesus said, 'Somebody touched Me, for I perceived power going out from Me.' Now when the woman saw that she was not hidden, she came trembling; and falling down before Him, she declared to Him in the presence of all the people the reason she had touched

23

Him and how she was healed immediately. And He said to her, 'Daughter, be of good cheer; your faith has made you well. Go in peace.'"

While at its conception, in my perspective, the song was about *that* woman, but ultimately, it was really about *me*; a woman with an issue pressing through pain to touch Jesus. In that same regard, it can be about all of us. We all have an issue. If we're honest, we all have many issues, and we all have something or somebody that could keep us from Jesus, but we press through the crowds, the pain, the fear. We press through because we know the only way to become whole is through touching Jesus.

My song is called *Run to You*.

Run to You

Jesus, my heart is set upon You
My Ransom, Redeemer, my soul's rescue
I cry out in weakness
You breathe in me strength anew
You are my everything

So I run to You
I run to You
I run to You, Jesus

Longing to be with You
Just to touch your garment
To breathe in Your holiness
I just want to linger here
Where all else fades away
And only You remain

In Jeremiah 29:13, God's Word says, "And you will seek Me and find Me, when you search for Me with your whole heart." And so, I have run after Jesus, seeking and searching, trusting that His Word is true and that my desire to be in alignment with Him will be honored by His faithfulness. Part of being in alignment with His will is writing this book.

My goal is to use what I have learned about myself and the Lord through losing Rich and help other people on their journey to healing and restoration. The path is not easy and is definitely not fun, but it is possible to be full of joy in the midst of it. If we are to truly embrace the *new thing* the Lord has planned, we have to be willing to let go of the old thing.

Letting go doesn't mean what we had and experienced was bad. Letting go doesn't mean we forget the fullness of our past joys. Letting go merely means that we are free to receive what our Father has planned for us now. If we believe what the Word says about Him, then we know what He has said about us in Jeremiah 29:11: "For I know the thoughts that I think toward you, says the Lord, thoughts of peace and not of evil, to give you a future and a hope."

If you are currently in the middle of a difficult season, please let me encourage you that the pain you feel right now doesn't have to be a lifelong pain. Maybe you're scared, and that is completely understandable, but you are on the cusp of a defining moment. I know that *with* God, all things are possible, and that includes you coming out of this as an overcomer. Your willingness to trust God through your fear creates an opportunity to inspire and encourage others. The power of your story is limitless, but only if you let God write it in its entirety!

Chapter 5:

The Three P's

His Presence, Your Peeps and a Purpose

I'd like to share the three tools I used, and continue to use, in my healing process. I call them "The Three P's":

His Presence
Your Peeps
A Purpose

Let's discuss these three in detail.

His Presence: Hearing from God

First and foremost, regardless of whether your life is the best it's ever been or you are barely hanging on, the most important relationship you will ever have is the one you have with the Lord. The Bible says that you *can all do all things through Christ*, and the key words here are through Christ! If you're on your own, things are iffy.

My best piece of advice for people who want to move forward is this: You can do things your own way, and it could turn out well, maybe even great, but if you want amazing — if you want an extraordinary life — you have to do it *God's* way. We as humans only see the *now* moment and even that is through our own human, flawed perspective. In fact our understanding is so limited that we have no idea what is even going to happen to us 5 minutes from now. *But God.* Don't you just love the sound of those two words together? But God knows and has declared the end

26

from the beginning (Isaiah 46:10).

God knew on my wedding day that our marriage would end after 14 years with Rich's death. He knew the day Mathew was born when and how he would lose his dad. He also knew that we would survive, and as cliché as it sounds, we would thrive. He knows everything about my life and likewise, He knows everything about your life. He knows you better than you know yourself, even when you are weak and tired and tempted to give up, but He believes in you. He knows the limitless potential you possess, because He is the source of that potential. To receive true healing, you will need to rely on God probably more than you ever have. You will have to accept that you *absolutely need* Him, and complete reliance on Him will make all the difference.

His presence is a vital tool for your healing process, but what does it actually mean to be in His presence? First of all, it means we need to earnestly seek Him. "And those who know Your name will put their trust in You; For You, Lord, have not forsaken those who seek You. Psalms 9:10 (NKJV). Let me break it down a little. Just like with every relationship, you have to invest in getting to know the person. You talk to one another. You spend time together. You ask for advice. You pay attention to how they do things and ultimately, you learn from them. It's the same with the Lord.

Prayer doesn't have to be fancy, it just has to be real and genuine. I have found that I talk to Jesus the same way I talk to my husband or my friends. My vocabulary doesn't suddenly switch to "Old English." It's just me and Jesus, hanging out, talking about, well, everything. I can safely tell Him anything I have on my mind, mostly because, though we sometimes choose to forget this, He knows our every thought without us having to speak them. So you might as well be transparent in your prayer life. Angry? Say so. He knows it. Confused? Ask questions. God is not surprised or put off by your emotions. He created you as an emotional being. So, you are free to feel whatever you're feeling and talk to Him about it. He doesn't expect perfection from His kids, He just wants us to spend time with Him and to use that time to grow in maturity and wisdom.

Likewise, as with other relationships, it is also very important to listen. A word from the Lord is probably not going to come through a burning bush, though to be honest, I have requested that. Can you imagine how quickly clarity would come with fire speaking to you? Talk about simplifying a situation! However, more often than not, the words of the Lord will come to you in the form of a still, small voice.

1 Kings 19:11, 12 (NKJV): "Then He said, 'Go out, and stand on the mountain before the Lord.' And behold, the Lord passed by, and a great and strong wind tore into the mountains and broke the rocks in pieces before the Lord, *but* the Lord *was* not in the wind; and after the wind an earthquake, *but* the Lord *was* not in the earthquake; and after the earthquake a fire, *but* the Lord *was* not in the fire; and after the fire a still small voice." I mention this so you know that you have to make a point of listening for Him. A word from the Lord can come in a myriad of different ways.

He can speak to you directly. He spoke to Joshua. Joshua chapter 1 (NKJV) says, "After the death of Moses the servant of the Lord, it came to pass that the Lord spoke to Joshua the son of Nun, Moses' assistant, saying 'Moses My servant is dead. Now therefore, arise, go over this Jordan, you and all this people, to the land which I am giving to them — the children of Israel. Every place that the sole of your foot will tread upon I have given you, as I said to Moses. From the wilderness and this Lebanon as far as the great river, the River Euphrates, all the land of the Hittites, and to the Great Sea toward the going down of the sun, shall be your territory. No man shall *be able to* stand before you all the days of your life; as I was with Moses, *so* I will be with you. I will not leave you nor forsake you. Be strong and of good courage, for to this people you shall divide as an inheritance the land which I swore to their fathers to give them. Only be strong and very courageous, that you may observe to do according to all the law which Moses My servant commanded you; do not turn from it to the right hand or to the left, that you may prosper wherever you go. This Book of the Law shall not depart from your mouth, but you shall meditate in it day and night, that you may observe to do according to all that is written in it. For then you will make your way prosperous, and then you will have good success. Have I not commanded you? Be strong and of good courage; do not be afraid, nor be dismayed, for the Lord your God *is* with you wherever you go.'"

Could there be a more perfect and encouraging setting of scripture to a person who has found themselves in a situation they never expected to be in? I have found so much courage in finding similarities in mine and Joshua's life experiences, but I'll dive deeper into that comparison later.

He can speak to you in dreams. Joel 2:28 (NKJV) says, "And it shall come to pass afterward that I will pour out My Spirit on all flesh; your sons and your daughters shall prophesy, your old men shall dream dreams, your young men shall see visions."

In Genesis 37, Joseph dreamed he would rule over his brothers. In

Judges Chapter 7, Gideon overhears two men in conversation about a dream that one of them had. The other, upon hearing the dream interprets it as the impending defeat of the Midianites. It wasn't even his dream, but God used it to speak courage into the heart of Gideon.

Matthew Chapter 2 records many dreams that Mary's husband Joseph had concerning keeping his family out of harm's way. I mentioned previously about the many pregnancy dreams I had, but there was also another significant dream that the Lord gave me.

It was nine months after Rich had died. By then Mathew and I were on our own and doing really well. Our worship team was going to be recording a CD on a Sunday night and it was a pretty big deal for us. I'd been really involved in the process, and so was very excited. I awoke that Sunday morning with a dream from the Lord. In my dream, Rich and I were at our first house. I was in the front yard and there were three large zucchini plants. I was really excited by the plants, and so I called to Rich who was in the house. "Punky, come see what I grew!" Even now as I recall it, I get choked up about this dream. He came out, saw the plants and was so proud of me. We hugged for a long time and then it was over. I woke up with very strong and mixed emotions. I was so severely sad to have hugged him for the last time. His embrace felt just like I remembered. The feeling of losing him again was crushing, but instead I tried so very hard to focus on the message of the dream. He was home, and I was still on the outside of that, but while I am still here, I am being fruitful. While in the balance of hurting and healing, I was producing something for the Lord.

I was honored that the Lord would reveal this message to me in addition to allowing me a moment with my husband. I knew it would be my last glimpse until we see each other again at "home" in Heaven.

He can speak to you through other people. I've got some names for you: Isaiah, Jeremiah, Elijah, Miriam, and Deborah. These men and women were mighty prophets. They were the conduits the Lord used to give direction, correction and encouragement. Today, while we do still have prophets, it is more likely we will hear from God through the people with whom we are in relationship. If we are consistently in fellowship with our brothers and sisters in Christ, we have a vast supply of wisdom at our disposal. The life experiences and lessons learned by those in our lives can speak to us at a different type of relational level.

In Exodus 18, Jethro (Moses' father-in-law) gave him some much needed advice on how to better manage the God-given task of leading the people of Israel. While the words themselves came from a man, they were ultimately God ordained. I have found this to be very true often in my life. The Word of the Lord has come as a perfectly timed phrase in a sermon spoken through one of my amazing pastors. It has come through words written in a book (which I hope you find to be true for this book as well). It has also come through powerfully anointed speakers that I've had the privilege of hearing.

One such moment stands out to me specifically. I went to see Joyce Meyer with some friends a few months after we lost Rich. During worship I was a total sponge, and my heart and spirit were so hungry for what the Lord wanted to speak to me that night. Joyce Meyer has an extraordinary testimony, and if you've never been to one of her conferences or read any of her books, I highly recommend her. That night she talked about her past and how the Lord had told her that "Plan B" can be better than "Plan A" ever would have been." Oh my goodness! It was perfection and thus from Jesus!! My friend Crystal turned to me and said, "That was for you!" It was an awesome moment for me. My spirit was refreshed knowing the Lord has me in the palm of His hand!

The words of our Father have come through wonderful friends who are in alignment with the Holy Spirit. They have come as either specifically sought after advice, or just in casual conversation. Matthew 12:34 in the Amplified says, "For out of the fullness (the overflow, the superabundance) of the heart the mouth speaks." This means if you are surrounding yourself with people who are seeking the Lord, His will and His wisdom, you are bound to hear the Lord speak through them. I have been so richly blessed in my relationships! The women in my life are absolutely modern day Miriams and Deborahs. They have spoken and continue to speak Godly wisdom into my life, and I am grateful beyond measure.

Proverbs is full of verses urging us to seek counsel and wisdom.

Proverbs 11:14 (MSG) "Without good direction, people lose their way; the more wise counsel you follow, the better your chances."
Proverbs 13:10 (MSG) "Arrogant know-it-alls stir up discord, but wise men and women listen to each other's counsel."
Proverbs 15:22 (MSG) 'Refuse good advice and watch your plans fail; take good counsel and watch them succeed."
Proverbs 19:20 (MSG) "Take good counsel and accept correction — that's the way to live wisely and well."
Proverbs 20:18 (MSG) "Form your purpose by asking for counsel, then carry it out using all the help you can get."

Clearly we were meant to live life in relationship. Please don't let your fear or pain cause you to isolate yourself. Proverbs 18:1 (NKJV) says, "A man who isolates himself seeks his own desire; He rages against all wise judgment."

As tempting as may seem to withdraw and isolate, please don't! We are stronger when we are together.

He can speak to you through His very relevant Word; the Bible. There is nothing new under the sun. The people of the 21st century are experiencing similar victories and trials that the people we read about in the Bible experienced in the 1st through 4th centuries. We forge through hardships, loss, relational turmoil, financial difficulties, and illness just like they did.

I mentioned earlier about finding a resemblance between mine and Joshua's story, and I would like to expound on this. So often we read the Bible and feel distanced from the characters, but they aren't just characters in a fictional story. They were real people, with real pain and real joy! Because he, too, had lost his leader, I decided to do some studying, and take a long hard look at Joshua. While studying, I found so many similarities that it was hard to not be encouraged by his life story.

Joshua was the man behind the man for Moses like I was the *woman* behind the man for Rich. We were both happy to be in the background letting someone else lead, but that was only meant to be for a season. He lost his leader abruptly and was the one to take up the mantle of leadership for his *family*; the Children of Israel. I too, had the mantle of familial leadership fall to me. He was afraid and required a lot of cheerleading from the Lord. "You can do this. Be courageous!" I can't even begin to tell you how many times the Lord told me, "Sheryl, I know you are afraid, but you can do this. Be brave daughter! I am right here with you!"

Like Joshua, once I got over the shock of my new position and situation, I realized that my time with Rich—like Joshua's time with Moses—had been a time of training and impartation. Fortunately for both Joshua and myself, the people we were leading were open to our leadership. I had a long conversation with Mathew about waiting on the Lord. I told him that we weren't doing *anything* until we heard directly from the Lord. It is so easy to make decisions in haste when things are stressful, and I knew that wasn't the route I wanted for us. Then, I asked him if he trusted me to hear from God, and he said he did.

Joshua's family had equal amounts of confidence in him. "So they answered Joshua, saying, 'All that you command us we will do, and wherever you send us we will go. Just as we heeded Moses in all things, so we will heed you. Only the Lord your God be with you, as He was with Moses." Joshua 1:16 (NKJV)

Like Joshua, I knew worship was the way to victory. Every time I had made the choice to put my situation in God's hands, trust Him with it and declare His greatness over my, well, everything, I was successful. Mind you, success didn't always end up looking like what I expected, but it always had God's fingerprints all over it, and to me, that is success. Joshua chapter 6 documents how Joshua tangibly utilized worship as a mighty roar; a shout that brought down the walls of Jericho. It looked a little different for me. It was slightly less dramatic than with Joshua, but equally profound to the worshipper. I spent more time in solitary worship and bumped up my commitment to the worship team.

2 Cor. 3:17 (NIV) says, "Now the Lord is the Spirit, and where the Spirit of the Lord is, there is freedom." What's the quickest way to be in the midst of the Spirit of God and therefore have freedom from heaviness and distress? Worship! I believed, like Joshua believed, that if I was going to triumph over my circumstances, it was going to be through shouting, crying out, singing, and declaring the goodness of God. Because of the example of Joshua's life, I was also enthusiastically confident of *my* future.

Everyone knows that the Lord parted the Red Sea for Moses, but what many don't know is that the Lord parted the Jordan River for Joshua. Not only that, but God also halted the sun for Joshua in a time of battle; the only time He's ever done that. This tells me that his life *without* Moses surpassed his time *with* Moses. I believe it for myself as well; that what God has done for me and through me in the past, will pale in comparison to how he uses me in the future.

The way the Lord led Joshua through loss into victory spoke volumes to me. If you need encouragement, whose story has it? Or maybe you're struggling with insecurity? Then Moses is your guy! Overwhelmed by the Lord's calling? Read about Gideon. Striving to overcome disobedience? Jonah's life has some wisdom to impart. If you are struggling with who you were before the old things passed away, read about Saul/Paul or Mary Magdalene. The lives of these champions of the faith will challenge and encourage you!

The reality is this, if we really want to hear from God, He *will* speak to us. In fact, His wisdom may come as a combo; a God-speak equation if you will. This combo is when you hear from the Lord one way and then it is confirmed in another way. I have experienced this many times, but let me give you an example. One such time really stands out to me a couple months after Rich had died.

I was at the gym swimming laps. God had been silent with me for a while and I was desperate to hear from Him. So I said "Lord, please speak to me. We don't have to talk about anything serious." He responded, but the conversation was extremely brief and not at all satisfactory. He said, "But Sheryl, you *want* to talk about serious things. So just sing for me." I didn't like that answer...at all, but I sang. When I got home, an email had come in from my friend Shelly. She had been thinking of me and sent me a song that she felt the Lord wanted her to share. The name of the song is *You Are for Me*, by Kari Jobe, and one of the lines is, "You love for me to sing to You."

Wow – He spoke to me directly, and then confirmed His Word through a person that is special to me. Truthfully, He is God and He can speak to us however He wants to. His voice can come from many directions – we just need to be listening.

Chapter 6:

Worship

"Worship isn't an event to attend and watch. It is a lifestyle to be lived." -**Unknown**

His Presence: Worship

Most people hear the word worship and they immediately think of the 20 to 30 minutes at the beginning of their weekend church service. They think of the songs that excite, inspire and resonate with them. They picture the worship pastor of their church and visualize their favorite members on the worship team. However, for just a little while, let's take those forms of worship out of the equation.

Worship, in its simplest form, is believers recognizing and declaring the greatness of God. The question is, how does this help *us*, when it is, by definition, about someone else?

During a time of worship, our focus is on the Lord. We are acknowledging what we know to be true about Him mostly through personal experience. One of the things that I find myself declaring in worship consistently is, "Lord, You are perfect in word and in deed." Does the Lord appreciate this acknowledgement? I'm sure He does, but more importantly is the fact that *I hear myself* saying those words and know with all that I am, they are true. Whatever decisions He has made, they are perfect. Whatever words He has spoken, they are perfect. He knows all things and is causing all of those things to work together for my good. By proclaiming this, I am saying that He is trustworthy.

2 Samuel 22:31 (AMP) says, "As for God, His way is perfect; the word of the Lord is tried. He is a shield to all those who trust *and* take refuge in Him." Now that I have recognized He is trustworthy, the next logical step is to *trust* Him. When you are in pain, when it's the hardest season of your life, it may be hard to trust. However, it's also the most crucial time to make that decision. It is a natural, understandable tendency in a time of loss or crisis to try to control anything and everything you can. I get it, however, the hard truth is we control almost nothing. But here's the good news, we have access to the One who is on the throne.

Here is the progression we just went through:
God, You are perfect! God, You are trustworthy! God, I trust You! I know I can't control any of this, so I'm just going to give it all to You.

Through that progression in worship, we have freed God up to do whatever it is He wants to do through our situation. Let's break it down a little further…

God, You are perfect!

If you believe the Bible, then you already believe the Lord to be perfect. Psalms 18:30 (NIV) says, "As for God, His way is perfect! The word of the Lord is flawless: He shields all who take refuge in Him." It's one thing to acknowledge the fact that the Bible says it, it's something entirely different to truly KNOW and BELIEVE it in your spirit.

I can look back at times in my life, and see with complete clarity (hindsight being 20/20 and all) that everything the Lord did in those situations was perfect. But there is a key to understanding God's perfection. It is something we often forget: His perfection is *big picture* perfection. What He does and speaks to you may not feel good in the moment, but every circumstance will eventually fit together perfectly as He intends.

Let me mention this verse again: Romans 8:28 (AMP) says, "We are assured and know that [God being a partner in their labor] all things work together and are [fitting into a plan] for good to and for those who love God and are called according to [His] design and purpose." These events are all *working together* to bring about something amazing that the Lord has ordained. It's hard to grasp it, in this moment, when you can only see a portion of the picture, but God is in the process of creating a masterpiece out of your life! We know His ways are different than our ways, but why? How? Because He understands it all at a different level than we do. But why? Because He knows everything! He is omniscient: knowing everything. He is omnipresent: present in all places at all times.

In Isaiah 46: 10, 11 (NIV) He tells it like this, "I make known the end from the beginning, from ancient times, what is still to come. I say, 'My purpose will stand, and I will do all that I please.' From the east I summon a bird of prey; from a far-off land, a man to fulfill my purpose. What I have said, that I will bring about; what I have planned, that I will do."

Like an artist, God has a complete picture in His mind, but right now all we see is the incomplete work.

Looking back, a specific situation comes to mind. I remember being annoyed at the time, but now I can see why God worked it out as He did. A couple of years before Rich died, we decided to sell our house and move closer to his work. Our house quickly sold, and we found a new house to buy near his office. It all happened fast, but as we were preparing to settle all the paperwork for the new house, everything fell apart; the entire purchase.

We were upset, mostly because we had to move out of our house in a couple weeks, and now had no house to move into. At the risk of sounding dramatic, we were borderline homeless. We scrambled, and thankfully found a house to rent. It was a disappointing situation, and I was curious why God didn't work it all out for us, but at least we had somewhere to live. I look back now and can see that God had our future best interest in mind.

Had we purchased that house, Mathew and I would have been left behind, financially upside-down in a house that had memories at every turn. Trying to heal in the house we'd shared would have been an added layer of difficulty. God knew all of this and knew what we needed, big picture! Now we have a home where we've been able to start fresh, all because God knew what He was doing, even if I was bewildered at the time.

God, You are trustworthy!

We all have people in our lives that we find trustworthy. This trust grows out of experiences within our relationships. We have found these people to be consistent and reliable; they've proven it. They do what they say they are going to do to the best of their ability. Over time, these people become our go-to's. They are the friends, mentors and relatives we know we can lean on in a difficult situation. They are a treasure, without a doubt, but regardless of all of this, they are flawed.

Now, don't get all offended on behalf of your loved one and/or best friend! As much as our love for these people helps us to see them through rose-colored glasses, the truth is they are just people. They have limitations and that's okay! They are constrained by their understanding, their bodies, their emotions; basically they are controlled by the confines of their humanness. My husband and best friend both love me, without a doubt, but they cannot do for me, what the Lord can do for me, because He knows no such limitations. However, regardless of these limitations that I acknowledge, understand and accept, I still find these people trustworthy.

How much more so can I find God trustworthy? He is limitless in His understanding. Not only that, but He *knows* everything about, well, everything. I can trust Him to answer a prayer in the most exact way. He has proven himself to be the most reliable person in my life. How? Well, let's define the words trustworthy and reliable. According to Webster's dictionary, "Trustworthy" means able to be relied on to do or provide what is needed or right. "Reliable" means able to be trusted to do or provide what is needed. What have you needed more than anything else? Salvation. Talk about something that is *needed and right*!

In Matthew 16:21(NIV), Jesus tells his disciples what he would do. "From that time on Jesus began to explain to his disciples that he must go to Jerusalem and suffer many things at the hands of the elders, the chief priests and the teachers of the law, and that he must be killed and on the third day be raised to life." Then in Romans 4:25 (NIV) it is confirmed that he kept His Word: "He was delivered over to death for our sins and was raised to life for our justification." If it was through this act alone, I could find him trustworthy, but his reliability didn't end there.

He has made and kept promises to me for my entire life. It is not just our history together that declares Him authentically

41

dependable and trustworthy, it is also our present. In our relationship today I find absolute truth and awake everyday knowing I have built my house upon an unwavering Rock. I know that while it's easy to focus on our own suffering, the truth is, nothing about *our* circumstances changes *anything* about God. So, regardless of the storms that come, I know I can be confident in whom I have built my "house" and life upon.

In Matthew 7:24 (NKJV), Jesus declares, "Therefore whoever hears these sayings of Mine, and does them, I will liken him to a wise man who built his house on the rock: and the rain descended, the floods came, and the winds blew and beat on that house; and it did not fall, for it was founded on the rock." If you take all of this into consideration, I think we can agree that Jesus is indeed the definition of the word "trustworthy."

God, I trust You. I know I can't control any of this so I am going to give it to You.

If life were a courtroom television drama, this would be the scene where the judge says, "Lady Forewoman, have you reached a verdict?" All the evidence is in. It all supports the fact that God can be trusted, but what is the final decision? It can be hard, I know. In fact, it's the toughest part because it's where the rubber meets the road. If you say you trust God, then it's kind of expected that you *actually will* trust Him; not just in word, but in action.

In worship, we are constantly acknowledging the awesomeness of God, His power, His love, and His ability to do above and beyond what we can think or imagine. The unspoken statement in worship is that we are nowhere near able to do what the Lord can. Everything about us falls short when measured against the awesomeness of our God. Yes, we are made in His image, and yes the power of the Holy Spirit lives within us, but we can't compare to Him.

Theodore Roosevelt said, "Comparison is the thief of joy." If we are comparing ourselves to one another that is absolutely true, but if we are comparing ourselves to God, the exact opposite is true. We can actually find joy in knowing how much *more* God is than we are.

So what's it gonna be? Can you act on your trust in Him? It's a big step overall, which can feel overwhelming, but it's actually one huge leap consisting of thousands of small steps. So today, I encourage you to take one small step. What does that look like? It's different for everyone, but it could merely be something as simple as carving out a set amount of time to let go of worry. Usually when we are in trauma or crisis, it is all consuming; every thought we have is in the direction of that issue. Instead, try this: set aside some time to commit to something else. Give that hour or day or whatever you choose, over to the Lord.

This is a Biblical principal. I Peter 5:7 (NIV) says, "Cast all your anxiety on Him, for He cares for you." Make a conscious decision to say, "Lord, I have carried this burden for a long time now and the truth is, it's too heavy for me. I need a break so I am going to give it to you for this period of time, and I am not going to think about it at all." It will be difficult. Your brain is used to being consumed by this topic, so you will have to put effort into focusing on something else. Now that you have handed over your problem for a time, do something completely unrelated to your situation. Your best option is worship. Put some worship music on your iPod and go for a walk. During this time of worship your process will begin again.

God you are perfect. You are trustworthy. I trust you and I'm giving this all to you. Like with most things in life, the more you do this, the easier it becomes. In time, you'll realize you have started living the scriptures, especially this one: Matthew 11:28-30: 28. "Come to me, all you who are weary and burdened, and I will give you rest. Take my yoke upon you and learn from me, for I am gentle and humble in heart, and you will find rest for your souls. For my yoke is easy and my burden is light." A yoke is a device laid across the necks of draft animals to harness them together so they can work as a team. If you are yoked up with someone as powerful as God, the work will be light for you. You just have to stay close to Him and let Him do the heavy lifting, or pulling as it were.

Worshipping doesn't mean you'll stop hurting immediately. However, it does mean that you know deep down that God is performing a good work in you and for you that will ultimately bring about healing.

His Presence: Letting Him Change You

In times of struggle, Christians often speak of "going through the fire." It is typically a reference to either the story of the three Hebrew men, Shadrach, Meshach and Abednego, or the "refiner's fire."

The story of Shadrach, Meshach and Abednego is found in Daniel Chapter 3. King Nebuchadnezzar had a golden image of himself created for the people to bow to and worship. Anyone who dared to disobey the command would be thrown into a fiery furnace to die. Despite the imminent threat, the three men fearlessly disregarded the King's unholy command.

Daniel 3:16-18 (NIV) records their response to the King.

"Shadrach, Meshach and Abednego replied to him, 'King Nebuchadnezzar, we do not need to defend ourselves before you in this matter. If we are thrown into the blazing furnace, the God we serve is able to deliver us from it, and he will deliver us from Your Majesty's hand. But even if he does not, we want you to know, your Majesty, that we will not serve your gods or worship the image of gold you have set up.'" They were, indeed, thrown into the fiery furnace, but to the dismay of the king and all his soldiers, they stood in the fire unharmed, supernaturally joined by a fourth man; a man likened to the Son of God. This is definitely an awesome example of faith in action in the face of adversity.

"Going through the fire" can also be a reference to the "refiner's fire." The Bible speaks often of precious metals going into the fire to separate out the impurities, leaving a higher quality silver or gold. In the Old Testament, Job, in the midst of a devastating season, said this, "But he knows the way that I take; when he has tested me, I will come forth as gold." Job 23:10 (NIV)

David, in Psalms 66:10 (AMP) said, "For You, O God, have proved us; You have tried us as silver is tried, refined, and purified." We know both Daniel and David suffered greatly, but held firm to their faith in God. They were comforted by the thought of going through a fire and coming out enhanced and improved. If they can be encouraged in this thought, surely we can as well. While both of these references are encouraging, I would like to talk to you about going through the fire, from a different perspective…

One day I was watching a show on the nature channel about wild fires. I'm not normally a nature show fan. I'd much rather watch people compete over whose dish was the yummiest or which fashion creation makes the cut, but this wild fire show, for

45

whatever reason, had me intrigued. The narrator spoke of devastation, while scenes of a landscape, burned beyond recognition, filled the television screen. It was sad to see such loss, but then the tide turned.

He began to speak about something I had never heard of before: "Serotiny." Serotiny is the dependency on heat during seed production. What does that mean, you ask? Well, it means that seeds of certain plants and trees lie dormant for years until the resin covering their seed-carrying cones are heated, finally allowing a release of the seeds. The screen then flashed with a time-lapse video filmed over the months following the wildfire. Beautiful, green, new life began to overtake the charred remains of the forest. It was gorgeous. It wasn't exactly what it had been, but it was beautiful in a way that only new birth can be beautiful.

There are several trees and plants that rely on serotiny for new growth, but my favorite is the Sequoia Gigantea, otherwise known as the Sierra Redwood. Sequoias can grow to be hundreds of feet tall and over 20 feet in diameter. They can live to be thousands of years old. They are massive beings, born from an encounter with fire.

God spoke to me through this show. As I was watching this forest regrow, I realized I was experiencing the spiritual and emotional version of serotiny. My life, as I had known it, had experienced a wild fire. That fire could have completely consumed me and my relationship with the Lord, but instead, it brought about new life. This new life included new relationships, new experiences and new opportunities for ministry. I firmly believe it is the life God always intended for me, and though the journey was difficult, it is ultimately a process I chose to embrace. That day I had (and still have) great expectations of the Lord and believed for a future that was the equivalent to the Sequoia Gigantea!

I talked to the Lord about my high expectations. The conversation took place as I was driving to worship practice one evening. Mathew and I were still living with friends, and so the trek to church was over an hour long; plenty of time to warm up and talk to God.

On this night in particular, driving along I-5, I decided to sing along with one of my favorite artists; Crystal Lewis. She is an amazing singer, and I believe in practicing to people that are exceptional so I can become exceptional. The song I chose is called *For Such a Time as This*, written by Ann Barbour, from Crystal's album titled "Gold." In my head, Crystal and I are on a first name basis!

Her song talks of taking great risks out of a fear of missing out on God's plan. Yes, it's easier and *safer* to live a mediocre life, but the payoff of being brave with your Father is immensely worth the work. His plans are exceptional, and as I belted out the lyrics, "but if I turn away, how will I know what I have missed? Have I waited all of my life for such a time as this?" I knew that not only did I want exceptional and extraordinary, I completely *expected* it! Right then and there I had a defining moment conversation with the Lord that I think back on all the time. I said "Lord, this plan you have for me, (insert sob here) it better be big, because my sacrifice was great!"

More sobs ensued. I was being more forthright with God than I had ever been before, but we were going through fire together. If you can't be your broken-hearted, completely vulnerable and honest self in those moments, when can you be?

I heard Him plain as day respond to my expectations, He said, "It's gonna be big." I was taken aback. I mean, come on. I can comprehend *big* when a person says it, but when God says *BIG*? Now that's serious! To be honest, I'm still not even sure what to make of that, but I know this; I'm excited!

Every day I live my life with Sequoia Gigantea expectations, believing with every breath I breathe that God will follow through on what He has spoken to me; believing that the trial by fire released something that otherwise would have lay dormant for who knows how long…maybe forever!

Here is more good news to focus on while you are "going through the fire." Unlike the wildfire I referenced earlier, YOUR fire is a *controlled* burn. Another name for this type of fire is a "prescribed burn." This first means it isn't burning unrestricted or without supervision, and secondly, it serves a purpose. When something is "prescribed," is means it's recommended (a substance or action) as something beneficial.

We don't normally see the benefits of fires while walking through them, but if we have placed our lives in the hands of the Lord, *He* is in control of everything and (as I must repeat again) is working all things for our good!

Let's talk about the two aspects of the controlled/prescribed burn. First: It isn't burning unrestricted – it's supervised. The Lord is the One who controls the boundaries of the fire, but only if we allow Him to set the parameters for all aspects of our lives. Often times, because we are flawed humans, we get out of alignment with the

Lord and venture out on our own. I have done this, and if we are honest, we will all admit that we have done this a time or two. Speaking for myself, I'm not sure why I do it. First off, it never works out well for me, and second, I always end up going back and doing it the way the Lord told me to do it to begin with. It is always a huge waste of time and energy. I can practically hear Him saying, "*Silly girl...*" But, like you, I am a work in progress, trying to outgrow my desire to do it my way; explaining away my disobedience as a mere inclination to *just see how it goes if I do it like this instead...*

I liken this disobedience to pouring fuel on the flame. When we choose to take the reins back from the Lord, He *will* give them to us. When this happens, the fire is no longer a controlled burn, but instead a catastrophe waiting to happen. We usually get mad when the fire is out of control and refuse to acknowledge our culpability. But, there is an easy fix: repentance! If you have taken back the authority in your situation and are finally realizing that it isn't working, in fact you realize you're making it worse, say this prayer with me:

Lord, You and I both know I've made a mistake. I've made decisions from a place or fear, pride and impatience, and that was wrong. I acknowledge whole-heartedly that You know better than I do the purposes of this season and of my whole life, and so I am giving this all back to You. I want to be back in alignment with You. Please forgive me for my disobedience. Please forgive me for not trusting in You, because You are the most trustworthy of all! I will try to remain submissive because I really do want You to be in charge, not me. Help me to recognize when I am heading in the wrong direction and give me the wisdom and courage to make the best choices I can; all in alignment with You!

Let this all be for Your glory! In Jesus' name, amen.

The second part of controlled/prescribed burns to focus on is that it, like EVERYTHING the Lord does, serves a purpose! We've already talked about serotiny, but prescribed burns do more than release seeds in the forest (and likewise your life); they also destroy the growth of non-native plants, which if left unchecked, could potentially take over. The fire burns up the plants that aren't native to the area because they don't have deep roots. The plants that *are* native to the area do have deep roots, providing safety from the fire. These plants will continue to generate growth long after the fire has passed.

What does this mean to you? Some aspects of your life have deep roots due to your relationship with the Lord. They are the fruits of the Spirit listed in Galatians 5:22-23. "But the fruit of the [Holy] Spirit [the work which His presence within accomplishes] is love, joy (gladness), peace, patience (an even temper, forbearance), kindness, goodness (benevolence), faithfulness, gentleness (meekness, humility), self-control (self-restraint, continence). Against such things there is no law [that can bring a charge] (AMP).

The "non-native plants" are those things that are contrary to the Fruit of the Spirit. The two that had taken over the most ground in my life were anxiety and fear. They felt like an invasive ground cover; likely to spread quickly and constantly snagging at my feet when I tried to walk through. These are the two that I struggled with, but there are others of which we should be aware.

Native plants in a Christian's life:	Non-native plants in a Christian's life:*
Love	Hate or Bitterness
Joy	Despair or Despondency

50

Peace	Anxiety or Dread
Patience	Impatience or Rashness
Kindness	Cruel or Thoughtless
Goodness	Harshness or Animosity
Faithfulness	Disobedient or Fearful
Gentleness	Arrogance or Egotism
Self-Control	Wildness or Self-Indulgence

*(See Eph. 4:31, 2 Cor. 4:8-9, Phil. 4:6, James 5:7, Matt. 25:40-44, Matt. 5:22, 2 Tim. 1:7, Rom. 12:3, Eccl. 2:4-11)

Please don't hear condemnation in this! I am not saying that your life is full of "non-native vegetation." What I *am* saying is that the fire of this season can help clean out any and all things in our lives that were never meant to be there.

Like with most things in life, we have a choice. You have a choice. Is this fire going to run amuck and burn out of control, destroying you, or is it going to burn away the things that can damage you and release something in you that you didn't even know was there? My prayer is that you choose what's behind Door #2, because I believe that your future is a Giant Sequoia just waiting to happen!

Chapter 7:

Your Peeps

"It's friends that count. And I got friends."
–Anne Baxter, in *All About Eve*

No, I'm not talking about the squishy, colorful, sugar-coated marshmallow candies that we all associate with Easter, although I do really like those. No, the peeps I am talking about are your people; the friends, family members, and mentors that you share your life with. I call these people my "peeps."

You see, we are meant to live our lives in community. Remember Hillary Clinton's book, *It Takes a Village,* based on the concept of the African Proverb "It takes a village to raise a child?" We are all meant to be Village People, and not just to raise a child, but to help continue to grow each other through our entire lives.

My "Village People" are a pretty varied group of individuals, but they all have at least two things in common: they love the Lord and they love me! If you are in crisis, you will need your peeps. Yes, you read that correctly, I said *need,* as in, they are an absolute necessity to your healing process.

The Bible says in Ecclesiastes 4:9-10 (LB), "Two can accomplish more than twice as much as one, for the results can be much better. If one falls, the other pulls him up; but if a man falls when he is alone, he's in trouble." I know this may be difficult for some of you, because as much as I love spending time with people (I am an extrovert times infinity and beyond), I know that not everyone enjoys the company of others the way I do. I also know there are some of you who simply find it difficult to lean on other people.

There are a million reasons why some of us just aren't what you would call "a people person," but living your life in relationship is a Biblical principle. It is also sometimes difficult to differentiate between relationships that will help and relationships that will hurt. In relationships, there truly are the good, the bad and the ugly! First we will talk about "the good" ones; relationships that will benefit you and aid in your healing process.

During this season, it will greatly benefit you to rely on these four types of friends; the Jonathans, the Ruths, the Silas' and the Elijahs.

David and Jonathan

There's no way I can talk about the Godly benefits of relationships without this verse: Proverbs 27:17 (MSG). "You use steel to sharpen steel, and one friend sharpens another." I'm sure Solomon took one of his father, David's, most significant relationships into consideration when he made that statement.

The beautiful story of David and Jonathan's friendship is told in 1 Samuel 18-23. Jonathan helped David through severe crisis because he believed in him. But more importantly, he believed that their friendship, and what he could bring to it, was ordained by God. This commitment put Jonathan's life and relationship with his corrupt father, King Saul, in jeopardy.

Despite severe opposition, and a considerable lack of convenience, Jonathan was a devoted friend to David. In fact, 1 Samuel 18:1 (MSG) calls Jonathan David's number-one advocate and friend. He set the example of a faithful friend who put great value on the relationship. Through his love for David and appreciation of their friendship, he was able to recognize how he could assist David through a time of trial. In David's time of need Jonathan was able to prioritize the needs of his friend over the benefit to himself.

It is vitally important to surround yourself with these types of people! In today's social media-centered culture, it is easy to have a thousand "friends" on Facebook, but still be lonely. The treasure is not in the quantity of relationships, but in the *quality* of them. We've all heard the saying, "I would rather have four quarters then one hundred pennies." Though the math adds up the same, as it turns out, those four quarters are worth immeasurably more than the hundred pennies when it comes to friendships.

My friends Matt and Crystal are those kind of people to me. They didn't hesitate when I needed someone with me at the hospital, and similarly, without hesitation and asking nothing in return, extended an invitation for Mathew and me to live with them while we got back on our feet. They are loving people who represent the Lord very well. Matt took on the father figure roll for Mathew to my great relief! Crystal helped me take good care of myself, both physically and spiritually. Their children, Gabe and Faith, also welcomed us into their home with open arms, loving Mathew like a brother. What a blessing this family was, and continues to be, to me and Mathew!

It's in friendships like these that you find stability when everything around you seems to be falling apart. It is important to spend time with people whose company you enjoy and who you are comfortable with. These relationships will free you! You won't feel like you have to be someone you are not, while pretending to feel something you don't, because they already know you.

You will be safe to cry when you are sad, shout when you are angry or just be quiet when you don't even know what you are feeling. The comfort of the relationship can also free them up to speak into your life. Friends who know us well will often see things in us that we cannot see in ourselves, especially when we are blinded by grief.

Because we had already built a firm foundation, I was open to Matt and Crystal's advice, suggestions and exhortation. The wisdom and encouragement they spoke over Mathew and I was an invaluable blessing! Emotional safety and the liberty to heal in our own way and at our own pace is exactly what both Mathew and I desperately needed at that point in time. Praise God we had people in our lives that could provide for those needs. We lived with them for six months, and in that time, our friendships grew immensely. We had bonded through fire, and that is a bond not easily broken! Our relationship has deep roots and has been successful in bearing much fruit for the Lord.

Spending time with your well-established peeps will be vitally beneficial to your healing process. However, this is not to say the relationships you have with people who aren't yet "top level peeps" cannot grow in the midst of your difficult season.

I actually found growth in certain relationships in the six months to a year after Rich died. One such friendship is the one I have with Cortnei. I had known Cortnei for a little while. She and her husband Evan were people that Rich and I had just started to get to know, and though we hadn't spent a lot of time with them yet, we knew they were going to *become* our peeps. The first night I came to church after Rich died was the next Saturday. I actually call it "Peep Saturday" because my friends, whom I consider family, came to service with Mathew and me. The announcement of Rich's death was happening that weekend, and they wanted to support me through that. They would also help stand guard if the condolences became too much for me.

When I first arrived at church, our worship pastor (and wonderful friend), Trish, and our senior pastor met with me privately to check on me and pray together. It was then they told me that they had chosen someone to be with me while at the church to serve as a buffer. She would be alongside me for however long I needed. That person was Cortnei. It was so beneficial to have someone there with me; to sit with me in service when it felt weird to sit alone. We think people are staring at us in the midst of something, and then we try to convince ourselves that they aren't. But in reality, people *are* watching. They see us and think of how they would feel if they were in our situation or they wonder if we are going to break down before their eyes. Regardless of the reason, people are observers, so it was helpful to have her next to me. She helped me not feel alone.

Cortnei and I gradually began spending time together outside of church. I eventually felt more secure and didn't really need her as a buffer anymore, but she had become a friend. She and her husband Evan were now a significant part of mine and Mathew's lives. It was clear to me that God had not intended this relationship to be temporary.

When it was time to move out of Matt and Crystal's house and into a home of our own, Mathew and I went house hunting. The house we settled on was still under construction, and so was the house right next door. We looked at both, and fortunately we loved the same one, but we had an idea…what if Evan and Cortnei moved next door?! That would be awesome! We were seeing them that afternoon, and decided to present the idea. Over a celebratory

Starbucks drink, we told them we had put an offer on a house and that the one next door was also available, asking, were they interested?

Two months later, our two families moved into to our new homes, right next door to each other. I prayed that the Lord would knit our families together and He has done so in an amazing way. They are the most phenomenal "aunt and uncle" to Mathew and sister and brother to me. The truth is, mine and Mathew's loss opened the door to these relationships.

Developing this friendship was really in no way beneficial to Cortnei. It was borne out of my need for help, but this friendship has evolved into family. Similarly, our time with Matt and Crystal didn't benefit them either. Their love for us equipped them to help us without expectation. My point is this; you need people who aren't in the relationship for what you can do for them, because right now, you can't really do anything for them – and that's okay. You need this time to heal and be poured into. But, the key is to use wisdom and discernment in regards to whom you let speak into your life.

Naomi and Ruth

Another pair that believed in the power of living life in relationship is Naomi and Ruth. Ruth was committed to sharing her life with her mother-in-law, Naomi, even after she had been released from the family through her husband's death. Naomi, out of her great love for her daughter-in-law, gave her the option of returning to her home and people (the Moabites) or she could choose to remain with Naomi; an Ephrathite. Ruth loved her mother-in-law and valued the bond they had formed. She chose to stay with Naomi.

In Ruth 1:16-17 (MSG) she stated her hope of maintaining that bond. But Ruth said, 'Don't force me to leave you; don't make me go home. Where you go, I go; and where you live, I'll live. Your people are my people, your God is my god; where you die, I'll die, and that's where I'll be buried, so help me God – not even death itself is going to come between us!'" The change in her circumstance, the fact that she was no longer bound to the family, had no effect on her love for, and commitment to, her mother-in-law.

Often times a change in our life's circumstances effects our relationships. There are times when it's alright for this to happen, and it may even be good. Like in nature, a change in season brings forth transition and modification, and a lot of relationships are meant to be seasonal. However, there are relationships that can stand the test of, not only time, but also, serious change.

Relationships can be likened to the seeds in the parable of the sower from Matthew 13:1-9. There are seeds (relationships) that fall by the wayside, there are seeds that spring up quickly, but have no depth and so they wither just as quickly, there are seeds that are scorched and choked by circumstances and there are others that have fallen on good ground, have been taken care of and have yielded, and continue to yield a great crop.

My friend Jen and I have been friends for over a decade. We originally met because she and her husband were the worship pastors at our church and Rich was getting ready to join the team. Dane (Jen's husband) and Rich became fast friends. In fact, they became *best* friends, as did Jen and I. Our families vacationed together, spend holidays together; basically, we did life together. We were the Beck-Creeks, a family of seven.

However, with the loss of Rich, our family dynamic changed. We'd had a complete puzzle and now an important piece was missing. We were unsure of how that would begin to affect our relationships. But, despite the unsettled feeling that change and transition brings, both Jen and I, and the entire Beck-Creek family for that matter, were certain of our love for, and commitment to, each other. Our bond is very much like that of Ruth and Naomi. Despite the loss of what initially brought us together, we are still very much a family. Some things were definitely different, but other things weren't different at all.

This type of relationship reminds me of the seed referenced in verse 8 of the parable: "Some fell on good earth, and produced a harvest beyond his wildest dreams." First and foremost, Jen and I had built our relationship on a foundation of a mutual love for, and desire to, worship Jesus. Just like with Ruth and Naomi, our friendship had been planted in good ground. We had taken great care to foster our devotion and commitment to one another for a long time. The Lord blessed our relationship and had so much confidence in it that He entrusted her with a vision for me after Rich died. This is her journal entry to me of what she saw:

"Last Tuesday morning on our way back from the hospital (before Rich had passed), the Lord showed me a vision of you, standing alone in the middle of a broken path. The road had given way in front of you, and a huge chasm — a deep, foggy canyon — had taken its place. On the other side of this pit was a beautiful place. I remember it was literally glowing with beauty and I felt like it was singing out to you. I felt like the Lord was saying that He has an awesome plan for you – a destiny that is all your own, and that Rich was going to leave us to claim his eternal destiny. I knew that God had planned and orchestrated the events of the previous day, and that the amazing, beautiful destiny He had for you was part of that plan. I knew He understood how this experience would shape

you, and that He would use it to prepare you for the incredible destiny He knows is yours. I remember feeling like the canyon was impossibly deep and wide for you to cross alone, and God showed me a bridge, literally one plank at a time being laid under your feet. I felt like those planks were rock solid as you took each step, and you were able to look straight ahead in confidence. The Lord literally said, "I'm ordering each step," and the clear message was that He was preparing your way through this, that He was undergirding your passage from where you are now to the amazing place of ministry He has in store for you with the people, the resources, and the clear decisions you need in the moment you need them. They will be there.

Crystal (Krachunis) said to me last night that she had told you that God will exalt your worship. When she said that, I saw that bright, shining place on the other side of the chasm in my mind again. I don't know the details, but I do know that destiny involves worship, and that it's at such a capacity that your former calling — the place you were in while you lived with Rich near his work, your considerations as a wife and stay-at-home mom, etc. — were shifting to make space for something new. All around, my impression is that God is doing something new in your life in a _very_ _big_ way, and that He will clearly show you your way to this "big thing" one step at a time, without fear or uncertainty.

I also remembered my birth experience with Aslynne, in that moment. I felt like God specifically brought that to my mind to explain the need for this unbearable pain that you are experiencing. I know it's for a purpose that it's giving birth to this new thing, that it's making the space God inhabits in your life bigger at a very rapid pace. With the pain, He is enlarging your capacity to worship, to perceive things in the Spirit that aren't easy to grasp in a place of comfort.

Above all this though, the message I was given before I got to the hospital Monday, and the words God's been speaking ever since, are that He has *not deserted you. He is carrying you through this, and by surrendering to Him, He will impart sacred meaning to your life and your purpose. You will be assured that He has a larger and more perfect plan in the midst of your grief, and He will reveal Himself through your weakness and your weariness…He's right there with you, holding you up, and each step is <u>solid</u>. You will be okay; you will be even more than okay. When your eyes are blurred with tears, He will open your spiritual eyes to see Him more clearly. I believe this with my whole being. Our God is so awesome, and He would only ask for a sacrifice this big when His plan is to exchange it for something incredible and <u>awesome</u> in return…something we can't even begin to fathom. <u>I</u> <u>believe</u> <u>that</u>."*

In my time of severe uncertainty, God used Jen to reassure me that He had a plan that I could walk confidently into. It was similar with Ruth and Naomi. Naomi partnered with Ruth as she made movement towards the plan that God had for her. There are times when unwanted change evolves into a fear of the unknown. This fear can paralyze us, ultimately keeping us from making the decisions and choices we need to make to kick start our healing process. But, you have to get back on track, fearlessly walking the path the Lord has laid before you. Yes it's a metaphor, but it's a metaphor about movement.

The Bible says in Psalms 37:23 (LB), "The steps of good men are directed by the Lord. He delights in each step they take." He gives us the direction, but we have to actually make each step towards the goals and purposes. I felt secure in my knowledge that God had a plan, so when He gave me direction, I took the steps believing that even though I could not necessarily see where it was taking me yet, God *would* always have a plank on which my foot could land.

For Ruth, the change wasn't unwanted. In fact she had chosen it, but it was still a change. She moved with Naomi to Bethlehem where they were starting the next phase of their lives. In this new city, she was unsure of everything except her relationship with Naomi. When she encountered a person who would play a huge role in her future, Naomi partnered with her in the process of positioning herself for the blessings of God. The story is documented in the Book of Ruth, Chapters 2 – 4.

While my relationship with Jen is more like peers (versus mentor/mentee), she did walk alongside me in a similar fashion. She allowed the Lord to give me the directions I needed, and because she is my biggest cheerleader, she was constantly reminding me that I was strong and courageous. Her words and actions constantly spoke of her confidence in me, but more important than that, she continually affirmed in me that *God* believed in me. She encouraged me to keep my eye on the prize, helping me realize that I could (and should) take the steps needed towards my future.

Paul and Silas

Another relationship that you will find invaluable as an example is Paul and Silas' relationship. Their story is told in Acts chapter 16. They were traveling together doing what the Lord had called them to do and then *BAM!* All of a sudden, like a two-by-four to the head, things went horribly awry! It started going downhill around verses 16-24 (MSG). "One day, on our way to the place of prayer, a slave girl ran into us. She was a psychic, and, with her fortunetelling, made a lot of money for the people who owned her. She started following Paul around, calling everyone's attention to us by yelling out, 'These men are working for the Most High God. They're laying out the road of salvation for you!' She did this for a number of days until Paul, finally fed up with her, turned and commanded the spirit that possessed her, 'Out! In the name of Jesus Christ, get out of her!' And it was gone, just like that. When her owners saw that their lucrative little business was suddenly bankrupt, they went after Paul and Silas, roughed them up and dragged them into the market square. Then the police arrested them and pulled them into a court with the accusation, 'These men are disturbing the peace—they are dangerous Jewish agitators subverting our Roman law and order.'

By this time the crowd had turned into a restless mob out for blood. The judges went along with the mob, had Paul and Silas's clothes ripped off and ordered a public beating. After beating them black-and-blue, they threw them into jail, telling the jail keeper to put them under heavy guard so there would be no chance of escape. He did just that—threw them into the maximum security cell in the jail and clamped leg irons on them.'"

Without a doubt, this was a bad situation, and it's easy to just focus on the beating and the jailing part. But, what I want to you to ponder is the two things they had going for them: they were in it together and they were under the covering of the Almighty!

Let's keep reading the rest of the story where we can find our strength and encouragement. Verses 25-31 continue: "Along about midnight, Paul and Silas were at prayer and singing a robust hymn to God. The other prisoners couldn't believe their ears. Then, without warning, a huge earthquake! The jailhouse tottered, every door flew open, all the prisoners were loose. Startled from sleep, the jailer saw all the doors swinging loose on their hinges. Assuming that all the prisoners had escaped, he pulled out his sword and was about to do himself in, figuring he was as good as dead anyway, when Paul stopped him: 'Don't do that! We're all still here! Nobody's run away!'

The jailer got a torch and ran inside. Badly shaken, he collapsed in front of Paul and Silas. He led them out of the jail and asked, 'Sirs, what do I have to do to be saved, to really live?' They said, 'Put your entire trust in the Master Jesus. Then you'll live as you were meant to live—and everyone in your house included!'"

For me, the Paul and Silas relationship was fulfilled by the entire worship team at my church. We are a close knit group, and while they didn't feel the pain of Rich's death as acutely as I did, they experienced a loss. For some, it was the loss of a friend, for others, a mentor. We were all wounded, but we had two things going for us: we were in it together and we were under the covering of the Almighty! With the emotional strength of my fellow worshippers beside me, I was able to worship during my midnight hour and just like with Paul and Silas, the chains came off.

Having people in your life who are committed to worshipping the Lord despite the troubles and trials that come along is essential. They can sing with you in the jailhouse until you are no longer behind the prison's bars. Remember, though, worship isn't just about singing songs to the Lord. Worship is something that we exude. It is shown in how we represent Jesus in our speech and actions. It is in our thought processes and in our quiet time. It is in how we interact with others. It is in how we let the Lord use our testimony to bless others. *All* of these things, if done for the glory of the Lord *are* worship.

The people on the worship team came alongside me however they could, and while it was in different ways, the entire team played a role in my healing. I always knew I had access to the Lord's ambassadors.

For one friend and fellow worshipper, Kimm, it was to come over at the drop of a hat when I said I needed someone to be with me. She let me completely melt down while a fresh wave of mourning took over. Sometimes you just need someone you feel safe with to sit with you. We worshipped together. For me, it was in weakness and vulnerability, but for her it was in strength. For another friend and fellow worshipper, Beth, it was a reminder that God restores ten-fold. We need people to remind us of the hope we have in Jesus. We worshipped together through the Word of God, she spoke it with authority and I received it with a spirit of expectation.

I also worshipped alongside my friend and fellow worshipper, Sam, who let the Lord use his testimony of loss to bring me peace and understanding. I sought him out specifically, because, of everyone on the team, he was the one who knew through his own experiences what I was working through. I sobbed during our conversation. "Will time heal me?" It wasn't just a question. I felt like I was begging for confirmation that any day now I would feel differently, and that I would move to the next phase.

My hope had morphed into an expectation that my grieving process had some sort of well-defined time table I needed to be on track with. In the first month I should feel "*a, b, and c*," and during months two through four I should feel "*d, e, and f*," and so on, and so forth. Wisely, Sam said, "Sheryl, time doesn't heal anything. God heals."

It was truly an eye-opening moment for me. I could feel whatever I was feeling and that was fine. God wasn't on the clock. If I was willing to let Him, He could do whatever He wanted, whenever and however He wanted. A weight was lifted! We worshipped together through his testimony. Sam had bravely gone through loss and was confident enough in the Lord to share what he had learned. I was open to revelation.

In the year after losing Rich, due in part to my Paul and Silas relationship with the team, the Lord breathed new life and liberty into my worship. My prayer is that my freedom to worship both in spirit and in truth, both on and off the platform, was a testimony to those around me.

Elijah and Elisha

In life, not just during trauma, we should all have a mentor(s). In a perfect world and under normal circumstances, we should all also be mentoring someone else. But, during a time of healing, we may need to take a step back from that for a little while.

A mentor should be someone with whom we feel safe and can be vulnerable, but who will also challenge us to grow. This can, at times, be an uncomfortable relationship, but sometimes uncomfortable is *exactly* what we need! When we're hurting, we need to be in relationship with a godly person who will tell us when we are making bad choices or getting stuck in hurtful thinking. During this delicate time, a mentor keeps us from developing a victim mentality while helping us to grow in the Lord despite our struggles.

There are multiple mentorship relationships in the Bible. One of the most referenced relationships is the one between Elijah and Elisha. This relationship involved direction and impartation. Because life is different now, the mentor/mentee relationship looks different in today's society, but if done right, it will contain the same two elements: direction and impartation.

I have found it beneficial to have different mentors for different aspects of my life. For example, I have a godly woman in my life who I consider a mentor in regards to my home life. I am in relationship with another godly woman who fills the role of mentor for my area of ministry. Both women are pastors at my church, but more importantly, they are women I admire and have found to be honorable and trustworthy. Basically, I trust them to love me, but also to *tell it like it is*, even when I don't like what I am hearing.

As I mentioned, the elements of mentorship I would like to share with you are *direction* and *impartation*.

Direction

The Bible is very clear on the benefits of receiving Godly counsel. Proverbs 11:14 (MSG) says, "Without good direction, people lose their way; the more wise counsel you follow, the better your chances." And in Proverbs 19:20 (AMP), "Hear counsel, receive instruction, and accept correction, that you may be wise in the time to come."

One thing to remember is that direction, or advisement in a mentor/mentee relationship, may look and feel totally differently than it does in a relationship with a friend or even a family member. Our friends and family will often wait for us to ask for advisement and will usually take our "side" even if we are wrong. Solidarity is good, but it won't help us to outgrow harmful thinking or actions.

Good mentors will not agree with you when you're wrong. I had one such conversation with one of my mentors about my personal life. She reminded me of my goals and pointed out that some of the choices I was making were not in alignment with those goals. I would love to say that I agreed without hesitation, but that would be an outright lie. Instead, I decided that I wanted to assert my independence and decide something for myself without taking anyone else's opinions into consideration. Can you say *big mistake*! I can, because when I went to her later to thank her for her advice, I had to admit that what I had been considering would indeed have been a *big* mistake. A mentor's job isn't to make you feel good; their job is to help you to grow, and growing pains are just as real in personal growth as they are in physical growth.

Mentors will sound the alarm when they see danger or the enemy coming after you, or tell you you're making bad decisions. These "sounding the alarm" conversations will probably not be a good time, but try to be open to this. Remember, you chose this mentor for a reason!

Impartation

Impartation is defined as "conveyance: the transmission of information. Basically it means "I do it this way and it works. Try it my way." In Romans 1:11 (AMP), Paul says to the church in Rome, "For I am yearning to see you, that I may impart and share with you some spiritual gift to strengthen and establish you." According to the scriptures, impartation is meant to strengthen and establish us, which is why it's such an invaluable part of the mentor/mentee relationship!

Danielle is the woman I go to about life stuff; balancing home life and ministry, parenting a teenage son, learning how to not feel overwhelmed, etc. I admire the example she sets as a wife and mother in ministry. No one is perfect, but I have found her worthy of emulation in these areas. I call her, email her or schedule coffee time with her and she is always full of wisdom and eager to impart it to me. She is loving and compassionate, but will tell me if I'm not going about something in the best possible way. Here's the thing though – she doesn't just say, "You're going about this all wrong." She says, "This is what I have done when in your situation, and it has benefited my family. Why don't you try it that way and see how it works for your family?" Now *that* is impartation. I so appreciate the value she adds to my life.

The woman I have chosen to mentor me in regards to ministry is our worship pastor, Trish, who also happens to be a close friend. I very much want to grow in my abilities as a worship leader, and who better to teach and impart to me than an awesome worship leader? We meet to discuss how I am doing, and how I can improve. Even more valuable than those meetings are the times I am just with her while she leads the team or when she is with me while I lead the team. In this relationship, the bulk of the impartation comes in the *doing* as opposed to in a conversation. I watch how she does things, whether it be how she exhorts the congregation or how she communicates her vision to the band members. I, then, put her actions into practice, but in a Sheryl-like fashion. My goal is not to be Trish, but to learn from her by word and action. She has taught me so much!

Do you have someone in your life that is mentoring you? Are you open to mentorship? That's the big question, because if you aren't open to it, you could have the most amazing person speaking into your life, but it will all be for nothing if there's no willingness to receive from them. If you are willing, but don't know how to go about it, find out if your church has a mentorship program. If they don't have one (maybe someone [wink, wink: *you*] should think about starting one), think about the godly people in your life that you find honorable and trustworthy. Make a list of these people and then pray; asking the Lord to give you direction about with whom to build this relationship. It is entirely possible the Lord will speak a name of a person to you that wasn't necessarily on your list. If this occurs, don't be upset or surprised. Remember, He knows everything about *everything*, including what you really need, so be open to that if it happens.

Once the Lord has revealed this person to you via the Holy Spirit or a pre-established mentorship program, remember to be open and vulnerable because that is the only way this relationship will benefit you.

If you do have a mentor, or mentors, keep in mind that your mentor may upset you at times, they may even disappoint you because the truth is, they are human. Be careful to remember their humanity and show them grace. Don't put them on a pedestal, because a good mentor doesn't want to be above you, they want to be beside you!

Now for *the bad and the ugly*; the not–so-great peeps; the ones that are old and stale because they are leftovers from *last* Easter. Sure, they look good from outside of the package, but once you take a bite you quickly realize they've long since gone bad and are a belly-ache just waiting to happen! Will Smith, the actor from Fresh Prince of Bel Air, has said, "Look at your five closest friends. Those five friends are who you are. If you don't like who you are, then you know what you have to do..." It goes without saying that we are a product of our environment and that includes our relationships. Considering this, it's vitally important to know who is good for us and who is bad for us.

Relationships with people who love the Lord and are committed to seeing His will done in our life are precious. Now, I'm not saying that we shouldn't be friends with non-believers. We absolutely should be friends with people who aren't yet in relationship with Christ. In fact, it is our mandate. Why? Because it's entirely possible that we are the only Jesus they encounter on a daily basis. However, it's important that we don't allow non-believers to speak unbelief into our situations. While we are vulnerable and in need, we want to surround ourselves with people who will emphatically speak life over us and our circumstances. So...it's probably not a good idea to accept an invitation from the friend who likes to use partying as their emotional band aid, or to rehash life's difficulties with the Negative Nelly (no offense to all the positive Nellys out there) who will focus on what caused our pain versus who is healing it.

Because God clearly wants us to know who to be cautious of, there are many warnings in the Word, telling us of the dangers of being in relationship with the wrong people. Here are a few examples:

Psalm 1:1 (AMP)
Blessed (happy, fortunate, prosperous, and enviable) is the man who walks and lives not in the counsel of the ungodly [following their advice, their plans and purposes], or stands [submissive and inactive] in the path where sinners walk, nor sits down [to relax and rest] where the scornful [and the mockers] gather.

Proverbs 1:10 (AMP)
My son, if sinners entice you, do not consent.

Proverbs 12:26 (NLV)

The man who is right with God is a teacher to his neighbor, but the way of the sinful leads them the wrong way.

Proverbs 16:28 (NLT)

A troublemaker plants seeds of strife; gossip separates the best of friends.

Proverbs 22:24-25 (NLV)

Do not have anything to do with a man given to anger, or go with a man who has a bad temper. Or you might learn his ways and get yourself into a trap.

1 Corinthians 5:11 (NLT)

I meant that you are not to associate with anyone who claims to be a believer yet indulges in sexual sin, or is greedy, or worships idols, or is abusive, or is a drunkard, or cheats people. Don't even eat with such people.

1 Corinthians 15:33 (NKJV)

Do not be deceived: "Evil company corrupts good habits."

While you were reading those words of wisdom from the Lord, did they remind you of anyone? Don't know? Go back and read them again, but first, pray. Ask the Lord to reveal to you if there are versions of these people in your life and to show you who those people are. This might prove difficult. Some names the Lord may speak to you might be significant people in your life.

Now that you've had a revelation about these people, you will need to have a chat with the Lord about the relationship you have with them. This may be painful, because He may ask you to make some changes in these relationships. That could mean anything from stepping away from them for a time or letting go of them all together.

I've had relationships over the course of my life that the Lord warned me about in advance. Out of my immaturity and some rebelliousness (ouch, acknowledging that hurts a little bit), I disregarded His advisements. It was far from wise, and those are not shining moments for me. But since I learned the hard way, now when the Lord says, "No," I try really hard to listen and choose obedience. It is a decision I make because I know He loves me and wants the best for me.

If the Lord asks you to make some adjustments in your relationships, skip the fit, and make your peace with the peace He is trying to bring into your life. You can always rest assured that regardless of the varying degrees of difficulty, any shifts the Lord asks you to make in your life truly are for your good.

Chapter 8:

Your Purpose

"What is the point of being alive if you don't at least try to do something remarkable?" –John Green

"Purpose." Now that, is a *weighty* word! If we understand our purpose and are walking towards it, the word is heavy with expectation and excitement. If we don't understand our purpose, the word can be like a monster algebraic equation that taunts us and our lack of clarity. If we *do* know our purpose, but are not walking in or towards it, the word is loud and booming; similar to being paged in the mall. "Sheryl Beck-Nelson, paging Sheryl Beck-Nelson...I see you there hiding in the clothing racks! Come to the lost and found section so we can get you back on the right track towards your purpose!"

Basically, we can run, but we can't hide. Whether we are walking in our purpose, looking around for it, or running away from it at Olympic Record speed, the fact remains that our purpose will play a role in our healing process. Mark Twain said, "The two most important days in your life are the day you are born and the day you find out why." I believe this to be absolutely true!

But, how do we know what our purpose is? It's not exactly one of those things you can Google.

Search keywords: What is Sheryl's purpose?...
[Enter]...
No results found...
Hmmm...

There are a zillion books out there that want to give us direction on how to find our purpose. I really like *The Purpose Driven Life*, by Rick Warren. If you haven't read it, I highly recommend it! In it he states the five basic purposes of a Christian's life are (1) Worship (2) Fellowship (3) Discipleship (4) Ministry and (5) Evangelism. Those are all fantastic, but *how* are you and I supposed to fulfill those purposes? We're all asking the same question, but for each of us there is a different answer.

The things we are passionate about are directly correlated to our purposes, or to use church-speak, "our calling," and how we pursue them. I believe these passions, desires and purposes are planted in us before our birth.

Jeremiah 1:5 (MSG) says, "Before I shaped you in the womb, I knew all about you. Before you saw the light of day, I had holy plans for you: A prophet to the nations—that's what I had in mind for you." Here He is speaking to Jeremiah, but since He is no respecter of persons, I believe that statement is true for everyone. He knew you, and the plans He had for you before you were even born! That means He created you specifically to fulfill those plans and purposes.

The evidence of those plans probably started to show up in us as children. What were we like as carefree little ones before we allowed fear, self-consciousness and other people to dictate our speech and actions? Were you an outgoing "star of the show" type, or a quiet, thoughtful watcher? Did you sing and dance and put on shows for your family or did you prefer and excel in sports, and lots of them? Did you write stories? Did you love science? Were you an artist? Who were you as a child?

The answer to that question will most likely represent our truest self. I was an outgoing little girlie-girl who loved to sing in church. I was comfortable in front of people and leaned towards an understated sassiness. I was compliant (No, really! You can ask my mom) and didn't struggle with authority, but apparently always had a little bit of mischief behind my eyes. Today, I am a grown up version of that little, outgoing girlie-girl who loves to sing for the Lord. I am comfortable in front of people and lean towards an understated (most of the time) sassiness, and I value the authority figures the Lord has placed in my life. And, in case you are wondering, I do still have a little bit of mischief behind my eyes.

All of these things have tied into and helped equip me for my purpose. Because finding and walking in our purpose is such a huge idea, I want to break down our purpose discovery journey into small pieces. Before we can understand the big picture, we have to understand the building blocks and how they fit together. These building blocks are the Who, Where, What, When, How, and Why.

Who?

Let's start with "Who?" Who are the *who*? The *who* starts with God and then moves on to you. That was practically Dr. Seuss language right there, but like the brilliance of Dr. Seuss, the beauty of it all is in the honest simplicity.

The simplest concept of walking in our purpose is pleasing God. It sounds easy enough, but it can become difficult for us people-pleasers to set aside the expectations of people and focus on the expectations of God. 1 Thessalonians 2:4 (NLT), "For we speak as messengers approved by God to be entrusted with the Good

News. Our purpose is to please God, not people. He alone examines the motives of our hearts."

My best friend, Jen, told me later on that many of my choices were choices she didn't think she would have made had she been in my shoes. However, she said she had confidence that I was actively in alignment with the Lord, and so she was never worried about me. Because she had that confidence, she never expected me to do what *she* thought I should do instead of listening to the Lord for myself.

People with good intentions for you will speak their opinions and expectations into your life. This is valuable, for sure, but first and foremost you should be listening to what the Lord is saying to you. If people are saying things that are *contrary* to what the Lord is saying, remember, you are not created to be a man pleaser, but instead a God pleaser.

People-pleasing is something I have always struggled with. I want everyone to be happy. In the past, if the desires of people in my life and my God-given desires conflicted, I felt torn, asking myself, "Can I please everyone? And if so, how do I do that?" Just so you know…you CAN'T please everyone!

Before I realized that pleasing everyone was impossible, my exhausting attempts consistently made me crazy! I am continually working on this, and I thank God that I've grown in this area, *a lot*! The desires and opinions of others are certainly still valuable to me, but if I am confident of what the Lord has spoken to me, there is no need to feel conflicted.

Since the *who* is most importantly God and me, and people-pleasing had easily ensnared me in the past, I needed God to build my confidence. After Rich died, the Lord gave me a section of scripture that I built upon every day. I knew these words had been inspired by God for millions of believers who had gone before me, but in this season, they were *specifically* for *me*. I believe that every aspect of my life — in my season of healing and beyond — were represented in these verses.

The confidence that these scriptures were specifically for me gave me a focal point. I knew if I aligned myself with His Word, I would be in good shape, even if the people around me were not quite sure about my choices. Here is the section of scripture the Lord gave me, found in Isaiah 41:8-20 (NKJV):

"But you, Israel, *are* My servant, Jacob whom I have chosen, the descendants of Abraham My friend. *You* whom I have taken from the ends of the earth, and called from its farthest regions, and said to you, 'You *are* My servant, I have chosen you and have not cast you away: Fear not, for I am with you; be not dismayed, for I am your God. I will strengthen you, Yes, I will help you, I will uphold you with My righteous right hand.' Behold, all those who were incensed against you shall be ashamed and disgraced; they shall be as nothing, and those who strive with you shall perish. You shall seek them and not find them — those who contended with you. Those who war against you shall be as nothing, as a nonexistent thing. For I, the Lord your God, will hold your right hand, saying to you, 'Fear not, I will help you. Fear not, you worm Jacob, you men of Israel! I will help you,' says the Lord and your Redeemer, the Holy One of Israel. 'Behold, I will make you into a new threshing sledge with sharp teeth; you shall thresh the mountains and beat them small, and make the hills like chaff. You shall winnow them, the wind shall carry them away, and the whirlwind shall scatter them; you shall rejoice in the Lord, and glory in the Holy One of Israel. The poor and needy seek water, but there is none, their tongues fail for thirst. I, the Lord, will hear them; I, the God of Israel, will not forsake them. I will open rivers in desolate heights, and fountains in the midst of the valleys; I will make the wilderness a pool of water, and the dry land springs of water. I will plant in the wilderness the cedar and the acacia tree, the myrtle and the oil tree; I will set in the desert the cypress tree and the pine and the box tree together, that they may see and know, and consider and understand together, that the hand of the Lord has done this, and the Holy One of Israel has created it."

Through this section of scripture, I understood that the Lord had called me to this season. It was a rough one for sure, but He had a plan and a purpose. He was with me and would see me through. He would reveal things to me in His perfect time. The only thing I needed to do was to be in alignment with Him. God should always be the first answer to the *who* question.

The next answer is "*you*." Who are *you* meant to be? Think back to what we talked about earlier: who were you as a child before you allowed the opinions of others to define you?

Chapter 9:

Team Beck-Nelson

Awkward woman meets elegant man and voila!?

There is one decision I made along my journey that I am 100%, absolutely, without a doubt, certain of: the decision to remarry. I always knew I would marry again. This may sound disrespectful, but I knew within a month or so of Rich dying that I would eventually remarry. The truth is, I didn't think I would be a single mom for long.

In Isaiah 41 verses 19-20, the Lord talks about setting the cypress tree, the pine and the box tree together in the desert, and that they would see, know, consider, and understand together, that the hand of the Lord has done this. They would know the Holy One of Israel created/planted their trio.

I knew what this was supposed to mean for me: the cypress, pine and box trees were representative of my future husband, myself and Mathew. I knew the hand of the Lord was going to bring us together, creating something new for us. I didn't want to remarry so I could "have a man." I wanted to remarry, because I have always known that I am meant to be part of a team.

Team Beck-Nelson came together very quickly. I had consistently told the Lord, I won't do anything until you tell me. I won't go anywhere until you tell me and despite minor slip-ups here and there, I faithfully adhered to that statement.

Apparently the Lord had someone in mind for me; a man named

Larry, and because the Lord knew the outcome of Larry and Sheryl interactions had *big picture* significance, He gave me clues from the beginning...the way-back beginning, before I even knew his name.

I remember having a conversation with my friend and worship pastor, Trish, about 6 months after Rich died. We were talking about my healing process. Her exact words were, "You will know you are emotionally healthy when you attract someone like Larry Nelson." I responded back, "I don't even know who that is."

We did the normal banter back and forth.
Her: "Yes, you do."
Me: "No, I really don't."
Her: "Yes, you would know him if you saw him."

Turns out she was right; I did "know him if I saw him." He was the scary usher at church that I consistently made a point to avoid because of my against-the-rules habit of bringing my Starbucks drink into the sanctuary; a big no-no. A couple months after that conversation, Larry and I found ourselves in the same social groups and meetings a few times.

There was some mild flirting, but we were both so bad at it that it was hard to be sure! Before the clumsy flirting, the Lord had already spoken to me about Larry. "He is going to ask you out. Make sure that you are sure (if you want to proceed) first, because you could hurt him." The Lord told me this in advance so I would have time to really think about it. I didn't want to answer in haste and make a mistake that would hurt this man, or me for that matter.

When he asked me out a few days later, I felt prepared...ish. I ultimately agreed, but after an uncomfortably long pause and an unenthusiastic response that would never make it onto the script of a romantic comedy film: "Uh...I guess that would be alright." I'm sure he was perplexed by that half-hearted *yes* and I can't blame him.

It was painfully clear that neither of us had a firm grasp on the how-to's of dating. I'd said yes, but it didn't occur to either of us to give the other person our phone number, nor had we chosen a day to get together. Duh. Not the sharpest tools in the toolbox that day, but we eventually figured it out!

The following Sunday I approached him, and while I'm clearly not one for smooth lines, I figured *why not give it a whirl*. I walked up to him confidently...nonchalantly (he didn't need to know I was messy inside), and said, "So, I was thinking, after church if you're hungry, and I'm hungry, which we're gonna be, because come on, it's a long day...maybe we can go to lunch." I just paused and let the question settle into his brain.

It was one of the few times I've actually stopped speaking at the appropriate time. I might normally go on and on, having it become weird and uncomfortable, but not this time! Nope, it was awesome. With a smirk, he agreed that *yes*, he would indeed be hungry and that lunch would be fun.

After our church's last service for the day, he walked me to his car and I could practically feel the eyes on us all across the parking lot. I told him I would be receiving at least one inquisitive text before we were done with lunch, and was I right? Of course I was.

We ate at a nice restaurant in town (kudos to him) on the water. The banter was easy. Turns out we are both witty, clever and fun to be with so it was a "win" all the way around. He was wonderful, and while you'd expect someone to put their best foot forward on a first date, the truth is, he is consistently amazing. Did he kiss me at the end of the date? I'm not surprised you're asking, but a lady doesn't kiss and tell. Wink, wink.

We had been spending a lot of time together, and then a short time later, the Lord spoke again. Mathew and I were in the congregation during our Thanksgiving Eve service. I wasn't serving that night, so Mathew and I were able to relax and just be together during worship. Larry walked by, in full-on (scary) usher-mode and the Lord said: "You're going to marry him." And I said, "Okay."

It was a strangely calm moment, considering the vastness of the (albeit short) conversation with God. I didn't tell Larry about this revelation from the Lord yet, until he, also, had a similar talk with Him. It seemed too soon. I didn't want to be the crazy stalker chick that dated Larry Nelson for a minute and instantly wanted to get married, causing him to drop me like a rock because I was nuts and clingy. So, like any godly woman would do, I encouraged him to talk to Jesus about me. The Lord told him basically the same thing about me, and with the approval of the Lord, we proceeded with our relationship.

He proposed just before Valentine's Day, about three months after our first date. I knew the Lord had brought the cypress tree (Larry), the pine (Sheryl) and the box tree (Mathew) together, that they (the whole world) may see, know, consider and understand together, that the Lord's hand had done it. I wanted to give all the attention to God about the new thing He had created. So, while those close to us already knew, on February 13, 2013, I posted this on social media:

"I once asked someone wise, someone who had lost someone, if time would heal me. He (Sam Ortiz) said, "Time doesn't heal anything – God heals." It freed me. I stopped putting a clock on my healing process and just left it all to the Lord. Not long after that, knowing I was ready for what was next, the Lord brought someone fantastic into mine and M's lives. A wonderful, amazing, godly man who loves us, and in May, we'll officially be a family. We are abundantly blessed and amazed by a Daddy who wants nothing but wonderful things for His kids."

We were married a smidge over 6 months after he first asked me out. This was my Facebook post the morning of our wedding:

"It's a pretty big day for me...all because of Jesus. He can take our weakened selves and rebuild us into something strong and powerful. Ashes can become something of beauty if placed in His hands."

Now just as a side note, the speed with which Larry and I got married is not for *everyone*, and the only reason it was for us was because the Lord was SO CLEAR! I was not afraid to be alone. I wasn't on the hunt for a man. Don't feel like you need to rush *anything*. The Lord has His perfect timing, and the goal is to adhere to that timing, not to yours or anyone else's. Remember, when we do things our way the outcome could be fine, good, maybe even great, but if we want awesome and extraordinary we have to let the Lord do it *His* way!

Being a wife to Larry and mom to Mathew is actually part of my purpose. Being a wife and mom is part of my *Who*. Don't for a second discount the role you play in your family! I hear the word "just" all the time, but there is no "just" with Jesus! You are not *just a mom*, or *just a dad*. There is no *just a wife* or *just a husband*.

Moms and dads raise the next generation; there is no *just* in that. There is strength, honor and a heavy responsibility in that! Spouses aren't just husbands or wives. Husbands are the spiritual leaders of their families. Wives are the "helpmeet" (helper), called to encourage and strengthen their husbands. Never, ever, ever let the thought or idea of *just* take root in your mind or spirit. You are God-made and ever so valuable to Him and the people around you!

Wife and mom was a piece of my purpose; my *who*. The next piece of it was *worshipper*. This is true of all of us. According to John 4:24, we are all called to worship in spirit and in truth. For me, it means that I am called to be a part of my worship team at church. 1 Peter 4:10 (NLT) says, "God has given each of you a gift from his great variety of spiritual gifts. Use them well to serve one another."

"Serve one another" means within the body of Christ (church). My gift lies in the area of music, and so, from the time I was old enough to serve, I've always been a part of my churches' worship teams. This is a gift the Lord has given to me, but it is not for me. This gift is a gift meant to be used for the One who gifted it to us. It isn't just to have, it is meant to be used all for His glory.

Chapter 10:

Servanthood

"... any definition of a successful life must include serving others." –George Bush

Now, I have a few questions for you.

1. What is your gift?

It's okay if you don't know – we can figure it out. Ask yourself these questions and go with your gut instinct.

What do you enjoy?

Makeing people laugh and praying for people

What are you good at?

Makeing people laugh and praying for people

What makes you feel passionate about Jesus and people?

Knowing He is the answer His love His word His "WAY," is life giving now and for eternity!

Still stuck? It's okay. Think about some of the teams and groups in your church. Do any of them jump out at you? Here are some common church teams:

Worship (of course I'm gonna say that one first)
Children's Ministry (little ones)
Youth Ministry (tweens and teens)

Greeters
Ushers
Administration
Missions
Women's Groups/Men's Groups
Tech Department (audio/video)
Building Maintenance and Security

Prayer
Bible Study
Prison Ministry
Hospital Visitation

Do any of those jump out at you as being a good fit for you? If they do, talk to someone about that team. Perhaps you can shadow someone who is already serving there. And, while you are serving others, listen for the still small voice to confirm that spot, saying, "I created you for this." It may be a bit intimidating to approach someone about joining a team, but don't let fear hold you back. Be brave enough to take steps towards becoming who God always intended you to be! I know you have it in you because *Jesus* lives within you, and He is courage and bravery, personified.

2. Are you using it?

If you *do* know what you are gifted to do, I want to ask you this: Are you doing it?

You know you love children and children love you; are you serving in the children's ministry? You know you are friendly and people take to you right away; are you serving as a greeter in your home church? Maybe you're a man who has a heart to see the men of God's house grow in their relationships with their children, spouses and the Lord…are you serving on the men's team at your church?

John 7:38 (NLT) says, "Anyone who believes in Me may come and drink! For the Scriptures declare, 'Rivers of living water will flow from his heart.'" Note he said *rivers*. Rivers move. They have input and output – a constant flow. We are meant to be flowing; God pours into us so we can pour out. He didn't create us to be ponds. Ponds are scummy; merely full of themselves. Yuck! Which brings me to the most challenging question…

3. Are you using it for His glory?

If you know what you are gifted to do for the Lord, and you are actually serving in that area, the question is are you doing it for His glory? We, as servants should always ask ourselves this question. I ask myself this question all the time. In the area I serve, it's easy to make it all about me, allowing Jesus to become peripheral. *That* is why I need to challenge myself with the question: "Sheryl, is this for Jesus right now, or is this for you?" I'm not gonna lie, my answer is not always the correct one. When that happens, I stop and pray, repent, and ask the Lord to help me get back on track. I never want pride to derail me from what the Lord has called me to. He is not pleased by pride.

When your goal is to serve the Lord and people, pride is the fast track to failure. In Proverbs 16:18 (MSG) it says, "First pride, then the crash—the bigger the ego, the harder the fall." In Romans 12:3 (NLV) Paul tells the Romans, "God has given me His loving favor. This helps me write these things to you. I ask each one of you not to think more of himself than he should think. Instead, think in the right way toward yourself by the faith God has given you." Don't think more of yourself than you should. Be confident in yourself and the gifts the Lord has given you, but always remember that you didn't do anything to create them; they are all born out of God and His perfection.

After wife, mom and worshipper, next I am meant to be a teacher.

In fact, we all have something to teach. I have spoken to women about how to let the Lord heal them from trauma, and this book is an additional platform to expound on that teaching. I also teach in other areas of life. On our worship team, the entire leadership team has the task of raising someone up to replace us in the roles we have. I do this by talking through situations, through relationship and through modeling the actual *doing*.

What should you be teaching? It doesn't have to be inside the four walls of a church for it to be honoring God. Whether or not it is honoring to Him is only dictated by your willingness to be in alignment with Him and to allow the glory to be His. What can you be teaching someone? What wisdom do you have? Can you come alongside a new mom and teach her what you have learned while raising your child(ren)? Can you teach someone a new computer program at work that will benefit them in their job? Can you teach someone to drive? We all have something that we can pour into others.

Remember, we are rivers, not ponds. Don't keep your wisdom and knowledge to yourself; it is meant to be flowing out of you!

After wife, mom, worshipper, and teacher, like every other believer my *who* includes being an awesome friend, an honorable and trustworthy employee/employer, a friendly neighbor, an honoring daughter/son – basically an overall excellent ambassador of Christ.

Now that you have a better grasp on your *Who*, let's move on to the next question...

Chapter 11:

Where?

Moving out of your comfort zone

Ask yourself this: "*Where* will I be able to achieve this purpose the Lord has called me to?" Are you allowing the Lord to position you for the greatness He has created you for?

Like I've mentioned before, when Rich died, we moved in with Matt and Crystal. They lived a little over an hour north of our church. It was the perfect place for us to be during our healing process season. We were surrounded by our close friends, and Mathew was attending a school he was familiar with since we had previously lived in that area. It felt safe. It felt like home. However, I knew that everything purpose-related about our lives was going to happen in the city where our church was: Lacey.

We loved being with the Krachunis family, but I knew at some point God would facilitate a move back to Lacey. While waiting on the Lord's timing for that move, we still made the trek to Lacey for services and worship rehearsals. It was a lot of time in the car, yes, but more than anything else, it was an investment in what I believed the Lord had planned for me and Mathew.

Like most parents, I understood the importance of moving during the summer, making the adjustment to a new school a little easier. At the beginning of summer, I began the process of looking for houses and getting the funding in order. Mathew and I only looked for one day before the Lord dropped our new home into our lap. It was one of those days where you could practically see the Lord's fingerprints on everything. We arrived at the house only to find out that the company selling the house had *just* dropped the price by $10,000!

It was a brand new house and still under construction, so a representative of the company accompanied our real estate agent and us as we looked at the property. He informed us of the new price, and in my heart I knew it was a wink from the Lord. I could practically hear Him sing, "I've got the whole world in My hands..." I told Mathew "God just gave us $10,000!" We walked through the house, loving every square foot. Then, even though we had both already decided, we agreed to look at the house next door which was practically identical. This is the house that is now Evan and Cortnei's home. When we came back to the first house, we wandered around a bit more, studying the details. Our realtor made a comment about the flooring, which was mostly still covered, but we could see a few inches of the edges along the wall. She said, "I love the floors. They are like planks." I immediately thought of Jen's vision; how the Lord would lay the *planks* out for me one at a time as I needed them. She used that exact word and it wasn't a coincidence. It was a precious moment between the Lord and I.

In that moment, I knew I had made the right choice, and so Mathew and I agreed on what was behind Door #1. The only hiccup was waiting for the house to be finished, but that, too, was Jesus. A *new* home. It was obvious He was doing something brand new for us – something completely fresh. This home was to be like a new wineskin, bringing forth new wine. It was a tangible representation of the new life God had prepared for us.

I knew a lot of people were following our journey, so to keep everyone up to date, on August 18, 2012, I posted this on

Facebook:

"Packing up our life again. But, this time it's for a healed and fruitful season as opposed to a broken and healing season. If you have ever doubted Jesus, let me assure that every good thing you have heard about Him (He's perfect, full of grace, and loving, amazing and astounding in EVERY way) it's ALL true. Let me and Mathew be a testimony to that...always for HIS glory!"

Moving day was August 25, a week before school started. It was a day full of excitement, and to be honest, a little bit of fear. Mathew and I had never lived on our own just the two of us. Fear, an adversary to my future, was saying, "You should stay at the Krachunis' house. They will let you. You're not ready and that's okay. You don't HAVE to go RIGHT NOW do you?" But even louder was the voice of confidence in the Lord. It said, "This is going to be awesome! The Lord has brought us to this moment, and He will help me to be brave! Thank you, Lord!"

It was to be a new and fantastic chapter, so I tried my best to drown out the fear with confidence and focus on two things: the task of the day and the beauty of God fulfilling His will. I hired movers; a gift to myself and to all those people who would have helped me move if I had asked. I acknowledge that moving someone's belongings into a new home is right up there with root canals on most people's list of *things I DON'T want to do today.* I get it! I completely agree!

Our first night in the house, I heard *every* noise. It was a little uncomfortable, but I knew it was the right thing; the right place at the right time.

A lot of times we misinterpret discomfort. We think if it's

uncomfortable it must not be God's will. That is not always the case. Being uncomfortable merely means we're taking a step out of what we've always known; our comfort zone. Where do we grow? *Out* of our comfort zone. Are you seeing the connection? Let's look at some amazing, biblical examples: Jesus' disciples.

The beginning of Jesus' ministry on earth began when he was 30 years old and lasted for three years. In those three years, he partnered with 12 men. Two of my favorite *uncomfortable* disciple stories both take place on the water. In Matthew 8:23-26 (also in Mark 4: 35-41) is the first of them. In The Message translation it says, "Late that day he said to them, 'Let's go across to the other side.' They took him in the boat as he was. Other boats came along. A huge storm came up. Waves poured into the boat, threatening to sink it. And Jesus was in the stern, head on a pillow, sleeping! They roused him, saying, 'Teacher, is it nothing to you that we're going down?' Awake now, he told the wind to pipe down and said to the sea, 'Quiet! Settle down!' The wind ran out of breath; the sea became smooth as glass. Jesus reprimanded the disciples: 'Why are you such cowards? Don't you have any faith at all?' They were in absolute awe, staggered. 'Who is this, anyway?' they asked. 'Wind and sea at his beck and call!'

This story tells me that life with Jesus will be uncomfortable! They were scared for their lives — it doesn't get any more uncomfortable than that — but they were right where they were supposed to be. They were positioned in a place and situation that would show them and the world (through their story), the magnificent power and glory of Jesus. Not only that, but they were in a circumstance that would ultimately catapult their faith into a place it couldn't have reached without that experience.

The next story of severe discomfort is located in Matthew 14:22-33. "As soon as the meal was finished, he insisted that the disciples get in the boat and go on ahead to the other side while he dismissed the people. With the crowd dispersed, he climbed the mountain so he could be by himself and pray. He stayed there alone, late into the night. Meanwhile, the boat was far out to sea when the wind came up against them and they were battered by the waves. At about four o'clock in the morning, Jesus came toward them walking on the water. They were scared out of their wits. 'A ghost!' they said, crying out in terror. But Jesus was quick to comfort them. 'Courage, it's me. Don't be afraid.' Peter, suddenly bold, said, 'Master, if it's really you, call me to come to you on the water.' He said, 'Come ahead.' Jumping out of the boat, Peter walked on the water to Jesus. But when he looked down at the waves churning beneath his feet, he lost his nerve and started to sink. He cried, 'Master, save me!' Jesus didn't hesitate. He reached down and grabbed his hand. Then he said, 'Faint-heart, what got into you?' The two of them climbed into the boat, and the wind died down. The disciples in the boat, having watched the whole thing, worshiped Jesus, saying, 'This is it! You are God's Son for sure!'" (MSG)

There are a few things in this scenario that distressed the disciples. First, let's talk about the fact that they were in a storm, again. They were fishermen, so you'd think they would be used to being in storms out on the water, but maybe not. They seemed overwhelmed by fear. Perhaps the storms they experienced while living life with Jesus were more pronounced than the storms they experienced before meeting him.

It can be same with us. The storms, trials, hardships, or whatever you want to call them will indeed be more pronounced when in a relationship with Jesus. A little bit of "wind" here and there we can handle on our own; there is no faith required. We tell ourselves: "I can manage this myself. No problem." However, when a huge storm comes...now that's a different story!

To survive a storm like the disciples experienced with Jesus takes faith. Recognizing that you cannot save yourself is wise – only the Lord can calm these waves.

In these two cases, wild storms arose, but the storms in and of themselves were not the story! They were only the backdrop, providing an opportunity for the Lord to show Himself mighty on behalf of his disciples. The momentous part of the story was Jesus literally speaking peace unto the waters, or the fact that He walked on water and invited Peter to do the same.

From Zephaniah 3:17 (NKJV) we know that, "The Lord your God in your midst, the Mighty One, will save; He will rejoice over you with gladness, He will quiet you with His love, He will rejoice over you with singing." Think of it like this: the hardships we experience are like picture frames. We see them on the wall, but the focal point is actually the photograph inside the frame. Jesus working mightily on your behalf is the photograph inside the frame. The frame is simply the circumstance.

The next thing that was uncomfortable for the disciples was the "ghost sighting." Jesus walking on the water had to have completely messed with their brains! To see something that you know to be impossible would be the epitome of uncomfortable. The Bible says it caused them terror, but Jesus comforted them. Jesus will do things that will mess with your head. It is bound to happen, so you might as well just go ahead and make your peace with it. This is a man who uses gold as asphalt…His ways are clearly not our ways…

Then, talk about discomfort, Peter literally left his comfort zone because of an invitation. In verse 29 Jesus said, "Come!" meaning, come out of the boat and walk on water with Me. If I was Peter, this is how the whole scenario would have sounded in my messy-thought-process head (consider yourself warned!):

Sheryl as Peter: "He said "Come"…I think that's what He said. Okaaaayyy then. Here we go. I can do this! It's fine, I mean sure I feel like I might throw up at the thought of it, but I'm sure it will be fine! *Wait*, maybe He didn't say "Come." Did I mishear Him? Noooo, He's definitely waiting for me to come out of the boat. Look at Him – hand stretched out and all. Try hard to avoid eye contact with Him…dang, not working. Okay, I'm doing it. I'm getting out of the boat. Wait! It's probably really cold out there. I should stay in the boat, but Jesus is obviously waiting for me. I'm doing it! I'm getting out of the boat! One foot out of my comfort zone…Two feet out of my comfort zone…OMG!!! I am *walking* on water! Look at me! I'm with Jesus! I'm with Jesus, and we are walking, on water! Look at me guys…Ha! None of *you* wimps are brave enough to do this! Oh gosh, hold the phone, those are *huge* waves. Oh no, I'm going down! Man down, man down!! Jesus! Save me!!!"

It's easy for us ground walkers to pass judgment on Peter losing sight of Jesus and sinking, but let us instead focus on the fact that he mustered up enough courage to actually *get out* of the boat. Certainly he was uncomfortable at the prospect. He was probably uncomfortable with the whole scenario, but he didn't see discomfort as the Lord's disapproval and neither should we.

Granted, there will be times when we need to use discernment, but I'm talking specifically about us using our discomfort as an excuse for not fulfilling our purpose. Even now there is probably an offer on the table from the Lord; an opportunity He is trying to drop in your lap. When it comes to the *Where* of your purpose, if He says "Come." You should definitely GO!

Chapter 12:

What?

"It isn't what we say or think that defines us, it's what we do."
–Jane Austen, *Sense and Sensibility*

Now that you (I hope) have a better grasp on *Who* God has called you to be, and to *Where* God has called you, the next question is *"What?"* With this question comes some self-assessment. What are you currently doing that holds you up and what are you doing that helps you to be successful?

First off, what is it that makes you be your own obstacle? Upon reading this question, you may be tempted to *accidentally* place your bookmark on the *next* chapter, skipping this section all together. I totally get it, but it would be a mistake.

While it's easy to blame a lack of progress on timing or who we are partnered with, or a million other factors, many times, the problem lies squarely with us. We get in our own way. I know it may be hard to hear, but here's the good news; we have the power to change ourselves!

Romans 12:2 (AMP) says, "Do not be conformed to this world (this age), [fashioned after and adapted to its external, superficial customs], but be transformed (changed) by the [entire] renewal of your mind [by its new ideals and its new attitude], so that you may prove [for yourselves] what is the good and acceptable and perfect will of God, *even* the thing which is good and acceptable and perfect [in His sight for you]." The Lord isn't like us, He doesn't say things just to hear His own voice.

When He speaks it is for a targeted purpose, so when He says be transformed, renew your mind, He means for us to acknowledge our faulty thinking, and then make the necessary changes. Some people say, "I don't need to change." Well, that's not true at all. God wouldn't have told you to do it if it wasn't necessary for your growth and success. If your mouth says, "I don't need to change." What your heart is probably saying is, "I don't want to," and quite possibly with "…and you can't make me!" next. If this is you (and you know who you are), then we know which thought needs immediate transformation.

Let's hit the reset button with a quick prayer:

Lord, here's the truth: I am not perfect. Only You are, so chances are good that I need to make some changes. I know I am meant to be a work in progress, and by not choosing transformation, I am limiting what You can do for me and through me. Please forgive me for not being open to change and help me to be more receptive from now on. In Jesus' name, amen.

Now that we are on the same page about being transformed, let's look at some areas where we may need to alter our thoughts and actions, allowing ourselves to make more progress towards our purpose.

What do I do that keeps me from being successful?

Fear. The first and biggest roadblock we set up for ourselves is fear. Webster's Dictionary defines fear as "a painful emotion or passion excited by the expectation of evil, or the apprehension of impending danger; apprehension; anxiety; solicitude; alarm; dread." In the context of my purpose, I define fear as an ugly box whose sole purpose is to confine me. Sure, it isn't as eloquent as

Love casts out all fear!

fear - thoughts, emotions that stop me from trusting God (others He's put in my life) keep me tied (to an old image pastor)

Webster, but that is what fear means to me. How do you define fear? *Then who Jesus has made (making me/us) to be -*

That is our understanding of fear, now let's hear what the Lord has to say about it. Believe me when I say that there is no shortage of scriptures about fear. The New King James version has the word *fear* 359 times. This tells me that it's a common feeling, but many of the numerous scriptures say, *fear not.* That tells me God never intended for us to be held captive by fear.

My favorite scripture about fear is Isaiah 43:1 (NKJV). "But now, thus says the Lord, who created you, O Jacob, and He who formed you, O Israel: "Fear not, for I have redeemed you; I have called *you* by your name; you *are* Mine…""

You are mine. Oh the beauty of those words – they sing to me! We are His. He loves us with a perfect love; a perfect love that will cast out fear (see 1 John 4:18). I don't want to assume you have fears. Maybe you are the fearless one who doesn't let anything limit you. If that is the case, praise God! However, if you aren't that person, ask yourself this: what am I afraid of?

If I am honest with myself in answering this question, there is one thing that I have made a habit of being afraid of: failure. Maybe I am just saying this to make myself feel better, but I think this is probably the most common fear amongst people pursuing goals, so let's talk about it for a bit *(a lot believed - foolish - natural)*

What am I doing that keeps me from being successful?

Fear - Fear of Failure. It's important to acknowledge first of all that no one has the "Midas touch." Everyone has failed at one point or another. Ever heard of Traf-O-Data? No, you haven't, which really is my point, but Traf-O-Data was a company that Bill Gates started with Paul Allen before going on to create the world-changing company, Microsoft. Thomas Edison failed 1000 times at creating the light bulb before he finally succeeded. Elvis Presley was told, "You ain't goin' nowhere, son. You ought to go back to drivin' a truck." Michael Jordan was cut from his high school basketball team, but his perspective is this, "I have failed over and over and over again in my life, and that is why I succeed."

Some of our most successful captains of industry, scientists, artists, and athletes have experienced failure's slap in the face, but they didn't allow it to define them or to get in their way. Neither should you!

So what if you fail? All that means is that you tried something and took a risk, and that in and of itself is progress! Eleanor Roosevelt once said, "You gain strength, courage, and confidence by every experience in which you really stop to look fear in the face. You must do the thing which you think you cannot do." We have a well-used phrase at my church: "Fail Forward." Like most things, I'm sure this means something a little different to everyone, but to me it means *freedom*. Even if I fail, if I do so in the direction I am going. My effort was not a complete loss. It's okay to *not* be perfect, but try something for Heaven's sake. Try!

The fear of failure reminds me of a situation described in Matthew 25. A master entrusted three of his servants with talents (money) to take care of in his absence. My focus here is on the third servant; the nervous servant who was afraid to try. He made the fear-based decision (fear of failure) to let his talent lay dormant.

Verses 25-27 (MSG) says, "The servant given one talent [about $1000] said, 'Master, I know you have high standards and hate careless ways, that you demand the best and make no allowances for error. I was afraid I might disappoint you, so I found a good hiding place and secured your money. Here it is, safe and sound down to the last cent.' The master was furious. 'That's a terrible way to live! It's criminal to live cautiously like that! If you knew I was after the best, why did you do less than the least? The least you could have done would have been to invest the sum with the bankers, where at least I would have gotten a little interest.'"

I don't want to disappoint my Master who has entrusted me with a purpose, and I believe you probably feel the same. So, if you have buried your purpose because you are afraid, then go get the shovel and free your gifts, talents, and abilities from their hiding place. It's time to put them back to work!

Your fear of failure most likely stems from a couple things; the first being past experiences. You are afraid of failing because you've failed in the past and hated the feeling of letting others and/or yourself down. Maybe you were embarrassed or physically injured yourself. It's okay. You can (and should) forgive yourself for that. Don't let it be an anchor that keeps you from moving on.

Instead of allowing that previous experience to be a pebble in your shoe, making every forward step painful, or even a huge boulder that blocks your path, take a page out of Johnny Cash's book. He said, "You build on failure. You use it as a stepping stone. Close the door on the past. You don't try to forget the mistakes, but you don't dwell on it. You don't let it have any of your energy, or any of your time, or any of your space."

Failure can be a stepping stone, but only if you allow it to be. You can choose, today, to renew your mind and set yourself free from

102

the weight of past failures. Remember, old things have passed away; behold all things have become new! Besides, if you *were* to fail again, (which, let's be honest, we probably will) the Lord is there waiting. He is waiting for His children to call on Him in a time of distress or weakness.

In Psalms 50:15 (NLT) the Lord says, "Then call on me when you are in trouble, and I will rescue you, and you will give me glory." And in Psalms 91:15 (NLT), He says, "When they call on me, I will answer; I will be with them in trouble. I will rescue and honor them."

Me, I have failed a zillion times. I have failed in communication by speaking out of anger or frustration. I know there were times that I failed as a wife to Rich, and I have fought through regret over those failures. I have failed in parenting. Good Lord, my failures as a mom could take up a whole book – just ask Mathew, he'll tell you! I have failed in ministry.

One particular time comes to mind; I was leading worship one night. The congregation was full of people deeply in love with Jesus and passionately worshipping Him. When that happens you really want to keep the momentum going, not disrupting the time the worshippers are sharing with Jesus. It's so important because in those moments the Holy Spirit has been given permission to flow freely in the lives of everyone present.

Enter Sheryl...everything was going smoothly, we were transitioning into the next song except, ummm...I don't know the words to the next song. I mean sure I totally knew it during rehearsal, but now? When it really matters? The words "I got nuthin'!" come to mind. Out loud I was ad-libbing and exhorting.

In my head I was thinking "I'm sure it will come to me….Dear Lord, it's not coming to me!!" I finally had to ask for the words, hoping that I wasn't disrupting the flow of the Holy Spirit. Ugh! You name the situation; I have probably screwed it up somehow. But that's ok, I don't care! Today is a new day! A new day that is covered by the love and grace of my Father! That fact is confirmed to me in Lamentations 3:22-23 (VOICE). "How enduring is God's loyal love; the Eternal has inexhaustible compassion. Here they are, every morning, new! Your faithfulness, God, is as broad as the day." Besides, what we perceive to be a failure can also be looked at as a learning opportunity. In fact, for our own mental health and well-being we should put on the rose-colored glasses that transform an "I screwed up!" into a "Now I know what NOT to do."

The other thing that feeds our fear of failure is pride. Ouch! I know, it hurts. In fact I'm a little bruised by it too, but it's the truth. We allow a fear of failure to dictate our progress towards our goals, because we think that our success lives and dies with us. Not so! The truth is we are merely the instrument the Lord uses to perform His will here on earth. You are a violin. On your own; silent. However, in the hands of the Master violinist who also happens to be the Creator of the violin, beautiful music is made.

Out of nowhere, the notes all fit together creating something extraordinary and wonderful. All responsibility for the creation of that melody lies with the one playing the instrument, not the instrument itself. It is the same with you. You are destined to bring forth something glorious, but it will all come through the hands of the Master. Your part is just to make yourself available and *keep* yourself available.

What does that mean? Well, for a musical instrument to be available to be played it must be cleaned, polished and restrung. From a spiritual standpoint, we first need to repent; the equivalent to being cleaned.

Acts 3:19 (NLT) says, "Now repent of your sins and turn to God, so that your sins may be wiped away." Next comes the polishing. This equates to our need to bring God our best by living a holy life.

Philippians 2:15 (NLT) tells us, "So that no one can criticize you, live clean, innocent lives as children of God, shining like bright lights in a world full of crooked and perverse people."

Also, we need to be open to the Lord making changes in our lives; this is comparable to being restrung. This may include anything from changing our relationships, our job or even to something as seemingly innocuous as our diet.

In John 15:2 (VOICE), John, one of Jesus' favorite disciples said, "My Father examines every branch in Me and cuts away those who do not bear fruit. He leaves those bearing fruit and carefully prunes them so that they will bear more fruit."

We take care of these three things and the Master orchestrates the rest. As the extravagant violin, you needn't fret (pun intended), because as it turns out, violins (unlike many other stringed instruments) do not have frets! Coincidence? I think not!

Let me give you examples of how to be the instrument. Have you ever been in a situation where you needed to have a conversation with someone, but you didn't really know how to go about it? You were at a loss for what to say or how to even bring up the subject. You were totally sweatin' it, but you scheduled the meeting anyway. When the moment arrived, suddenly, inexplicably, you knew exactly what you needed to say and exactly how to say it in a way that they would receive it!

This kind of thing happens to me all the time, and when it does, I always tell people, "That was totally Jesus! If I ever say something that seems really smart, it is absolutely from the Lord!" Perhaps you've had an experience where you felt like the Lord wanted you to go somewhere, but you couldn't afford it, and then all of a sudden a check came in the mail. That is the Lord taking responsibility for the things He wants to see achieved in your life.

Next time you fear failure because *you* may not be able to accomplish something, be encouraged by what Philippians 2:13 (AMP) tells us, "[Not in your own strength] for it is God Who is all the while effectually at work in you [energizing and creating in you the power and desire], both to will and to work for His good pleasure and satisfaction and delight."

So, when fear of failure rears its ugly head, tell yourself this: I am merely an instrument, an imperfect human in the Master's hands. I will do my part and He will do His part. Regardless of the outcome, as long as I am obedient to His call, I have indeed been successful, even if I do stumble while walking off the platform. That outlook pretty much sums up a day in the life of Sheryl Beck-Nelson.

What am I doing that *is* helping me be successful?

Taking Care of Myself. To be successful in anything your first priority needs to be taking care of yourself. This includes your body, mind, and spirit. If I were a flight attendant, I may give you this instruction: *in case there is a loss in cabin pressure, oxygen masks will deploy from the ceiling compartment located above you...fasten it so it covers your mouth and nose. Breathe normally. Please make sure to secure your own mask before assisting others.*

We need to make sure that we're prepared for whatever the Lord calls us to do. Keeping ourselves strong, physically, mentally, and spiritually definitely helps. The Bible says that we are to be ready *in season and out of season*, which basically means be ready for His call all the time.

Let's talk about wise habits of taking care of yourself. I'm taking it for granted that you are doing these things, but sometimes during grief, our self-care gets off track. If you are off track right now, then I'm going to use this section as an opportunity to apply a biblical principle taught to us in Romans 4:17; calling those things which do not exist as though they do...

First off, your body needs care. If we are getting enough rest, eating right and exercising this will be extremely beneficial. Whatever the Lord calls us to, we will need energy. It doesn't matter what it is He has planned for us, we will need our bodies for it.

Listening to our bodies is a huge step in the right direction. If I am tired, I rest. If I am hungry, I eat something healthy. But, can I just tell you that I have to remind myself of this *all the time*! Hi. My name is Sheryl and I am a chip-aholic. If it was even marginally healthy (truth be told, I would settle for *if it wasn't bad for me*) and socially acceptable, I would probably have chips and guacamole for dinner at least one night a week. But "Noooooooo, that's not good for me," she said with a roll of the eyes! That's the food

107

pyramid turned upside down, then knocked over and kicked a few times. And so, instead I try to eat healthy meals...sometimes with chips and guacamole *on the side!*

It's also wise to make time for exercise. Exercise increases our physical endurance. I'm not saying we can't achieve God's purposes if we are unhealthy, but it will just be so much easier if we are! If you're a singer or a speaker like me, take care of your voice, it is your most valuable instrument and tool. If you're a musician, keep your muscles strong so you can play to the best of your ability. If you serve with children, you will definitely need to be healthy just so you can keep up with them! If you are a greeter or usher, you stand *a lot*, so your legs need to be strong. Basically, what I'm saying is we will have a much easier time fulfilling our purpose if our bodies are healthy and strong.

Next, is caring for your mind...it's a terrible thing to waste. Don't waste it! Instead, increase your knowledge. Proverbs 10:14a (NIV) says, "The wise store up knowledge." Proverbs 18:15 (VOICE) tells us that, "Clever people go after knowledge to obtain it, and wise people attune their ears to hear it." Since none of us *have arrived* at an all-knowing level, we should be in a constant state of learning. There are a myriad of ways to learn and keep learning. Read books. Take a class. Ask someone to teach you something new. There are so many things to learn and so many ways to go about it. For musicians and singers, there are instrumental and vocal lessons. There are schools galore; online, public, private, and subject specific! My church has a program called Formation School of Leaders. It includes classes on the Bible, worship, leadership, and more. I took the leadership class, graciously taught by my senior pastor. It was a fantastic time of learning and growing.

Don't have time for a class? There is a book to teach you pretty much anything you are interested in, just ask Amazon. Problem solved! I love this Chinese Proverb: "Learning is like rowing upstream: not to advance is to drop back." We don't want to go backwards, so we must always be putting effort forward into increasing our knowledge through learning.

Lastly, you need to take care of your spirit. Ever hear the phrase "Garbage in – garbage out?" It's true. Whatever you feed your spirit is reflected in what you give out. The Word says in Matthew 12:34b (NKJV), "For out of the abundance of the heart the mouth speaks."

Are you being careful about what you feed your spirit? What are you watching? What are you reading? In what types of conversations are you participating? All of these things feed your spirit. I know a lot people like horror movies, but I just can't do it. They are too scary for me, and I don't want to put anything in my spirit that breeds fear. Jesus is anti-fear, so I am anti-fear, plus I'm a little bit of a baby about those kinds of things.

Besides questionable movies, there are a lot of books out there that are pretty risqué. It's almost like "dirty" has become its own genre. I tried to read one. Ummm…can you say *uncomfortable*? Normally, I might pass a book on to someone else, but instead I threw it away. It really did belong in the garbage instead of inside my spirit.

Conversations that focus on the negative are draining, and I'll be honest, make me annoyed. And gossip? We all know it's bad, but did you know that the Word talks about it quite a bit? Yes, in Proverbs 16:28 (TLB) it says, "An evil man sows strife; gossip separates the best of friends." You don't want to hang out with people like that and you definitely don't want to *be* that person, so be very careful about your conversations.

None of these things are good for our spirits, so it's best if we purposefully try to steer clear of them. Instead, we can watch, read, speak about, and think on things that are "true, noble, reputable, authentic, compelling, gracious — the best, not the worst; the beautiful, not the ugly; things to praise, not things to curse" as instructed to us in Philippians 4:8 (MSG). Thinking on lovely things can be a vague notion and it will look differently for everyone, but there are a few things that work really well for me. If I'm feeling anxious, I sing to myself. There is one song in particular that is my go-to song in a time of worry. It's called *Peace Speaker* written by Geron Davis. My favorite part says:

> *I know the Peace Speaker, I know Him by Name*
> *I know the Peace Speaker, He controls the wind and the waves*
> *When He says, "Peace, be still," they have to obey*
> *I know the Peace Speaker, Yes, I know Him by Name*

That song helps me to think on the loveliness of God's peace. If I am feeling blah, I like to partake of something creative. For me, that means (hold the judgment) watching cooking or fashion design shows. Seeing people make something out of nothing sparks something magical in my brain. Creativity is lovely, and it inspires me out of my doldrums.

What am I doing that *is* helping me be successful?

Practice and Preparation. You and I both know that nobody wakes up one morning, says, "I'm going to be a concert pianist," and then, that day, sweeps the nation with their unimaginable talent. Not one single athlete chose their sport and then immediately was ready for the Hall of Fame. Nope. It takes work. It takes practice and preparation.

Joyce Meyer said, "The way anything is developed is through practice, practice, practice, practice, practice, practice, practice, practice, practice, and more practice." She is so right. To become excellent, we need to practice and prepare. If God has called you to change the world through excelling in a sport, you get up in the morning and go practice. You invest your efforts in sprints and drills. If your purpose is tied to public speaking, you rehearse your speech over and over before you get to the venue. You record yourself to hear how you sound, checking to see what needs to be tweaked. Musicians practice scales and then move on to the songs they will perform. Rich was an excellent guitar player. In fact, people still talk to me about how awesome he was at his instrument. My answer is always the same; "He was awesome because he practiced all the time." He cared very much about giving God his best, so he spent a lot of time in preparation.

Just like dieting, becoming excellent isn't an overnight process. It requires commitment and diligence towards a goal. Then, once you meet the goal, celebrate! But, don't stop there. Always have a more challenging goal in mind – the next level. The path to excellence is most definitely not for the faint of heart, but out of our deep love for Jesus, that is exactly what we want to give Him!

What am I doing that *is* helping me be successful?

Training up the Next Generation. In regards to fulfilling our purpose, it's so easy to focus on ourselves. I mean it is *our* purpose, right? I totally get it. However, if we keep the focus on what *we* are accomplishing, we will overlook a huge part of the process;

training up the next generation.

Titus 2 speaks extensively about the older generation living an honorable life so they're able to train the younger generation how to do the same. Because I value mentorship in my own life, I have made mentoring others a priority. For example, couples who've been successfully married for decades are a wealth of experience for newlyweds. Parents of adults can advise parents of teenagers who can, in turn, offer advice to parents of little ones. I think it's a pretty common practice in regards to home life, yet we don't always make it a priority in regards to the areas where we are serving.

Just like we should keep learning, we should also be teaching. My perception is that we often choose *not* to share helpful knowledge that could help someone else grow, because we are afraid of being replaced. This is a thought process that we have to make a concerted effort to change. Our goal should not be to be the best worship leader or teacher or nurse. Our goal should be becoming the best version of ourselves and to help others become the best version of themselves. We aren't in competition with each other for a spot or position. God has a spot and position for each of us. A better mindset to have is this: *there is enough to go around.*

Once we realize this and start to feel more secure, we can help develop others. I really enjoy my role of helping the young people, and people new to singing, develop their vocal skill on our worship team. We need to renew our thinking and realize that in the family of God, if *one* of us wins, we *all* win. Romans 12:5 (VOICE) says, "We, too — the many — are different parts that form one body in the Anointed One. Each one of us is joined with one another, *and we become together what we could not be alone.*"

Go share what you've learned, and in so doing, become a building block in the lives of others.

Chapter 13:

When?

Are we there yet? Are we there yet? How about now?

The Now

The next question to consider is *"When?"* It's easy to answer in haste and say, "Right now, of course!" but that might not necessarily be the right answer. Although to be honest, I respect your excitement. I would imagine the Lord hears the question "When?!?" just as often as He hears, *Why?* It's a legitimate question. There are a couple of variables that come into play in regards to *why* the fruition of something purpose-related isn't happening right now. We are an eager bunch, raring to go, but if He hasn't facilitated something, it's because it isn't time yet.

Ecclesiastes 8:6a (NLT) says, "For there is a time and a way for everything." God has *perfect* timing. His ways are higher than our ways, and often we don't understand His timing. Secondly, as eager as we are (no one is accusing us of lacking enthusiasm, that's for sure) we probably just aren't ready. We should, of course, always be fully engaged in preparing, but the timing and how it all comes together is all up to the Lord.

When something you've been dreaming of seems afar off, it's easy to lose patience and get into the "Are we there yet? Are we there yet?" thought process. Usually with the follow up of "Dad, how much longer? This is taking forever!"

When you feel these impatient questions coming on, remind yourself of Galatians 6:9 (NIV), "Let us not become weary in doing good, for at the proper time we will reap a harvest if we do not give up." Do you know what part of this verse is my favorite? The part where it says *the proper time*. This tells me that there is, indeed, a proper time, and it's coming. So, I tell myself, "Sheryl, just keep chugging along doing what you're doing, and when it's time, you'll be ready." This is really my only responsibility. The rest is on the Lord. So be encouraged! Keep doing what you are doing; preparing and staying in alignment with the Lord and then, at the perfect time, He will bring it all to fruition.

I know it's hard to wait. In fact, it's one of the hardest things there is. God knew as humans we'd struggle with the waiting process, so He encouraged us through His Word. Habakkuk 2:3 (TLB) says, "But these things I plan won't happen right away. Slowly, steadily, surely, the time approaches when the vision will be fulfilled. If it seems slow, do not despair, for these things will surely come to pass. Just be patient! They will not be overdue a single day!"

Taking that scripture into consideration, let's get into "hindsight is 20/20" mode for a moment. Think back on a situation when you felt like you waited for a painfully long time. Maybe you were praying and waiting for a spouse. Perhaps you were waiting prayerfully for a child. Maybe you were having faith for a new job or a new home. The wait seemed excruciating, but when it finally happened, you realized that it actually happened at the most perfect time. If it had come any earlier, some of the pieces wouldn't have fit together like they were supposed to. Looking back, you see how God brought it all together at the precise and perfect moment; the moment of His choosing. You realize that He didn't ask you to wait just because He can, He asked you to wait because He was fitting multiple pieces together for your good.

The other reason things don't happen at the time of *our* choosing is because we simply aren't ready for the next step in the grand adventure He has for us. Please don't think that's a bad thing or receive it as a criticism. Let me point out that we are meant to be a *work in progress*.

The Bible says in 1 Corinthians 3:18 (NLT), "So all of us who have had that veil removed can see and reflect the glory of the Lord. And the Lord — who is the Spirit — makes us more and more like him as we are changed into his glorious image."

He is making us more and more like Him so we can accomplish more today than we did yesterday, and more tomorrow than we did today. It is a glorious process. Just accept the fact that you won't jump directly from A to Z. There are multiple steps from the day of planting to the day of harvest. If any are overlooked or ignored, the fruit won't be as good as it was meant to be. It is the same with us. I mentioned before that we just need to keep preparing and stay in alignment with the Lord. In that alignment with His will and plan, we make the progress towards our God-given dreams and purposes.

I, myself, have had big dreams for years and years. I held them at arm's length because I didn't see any way that I could be that person that achieves those goals. They were too grand. You may know exactly what I'm talking about. While part of me wanted to dare to dream big dreams, the other part of me didn't see how the Lord could put the pieces together in such a way that they'd actually come to fruition. I am sad to admit that I tucked the big dreams away like fine china; proof in and of itself that I wasn't ready. I had packed them carefully and put them on a shelf, until the day the Lord said, "Sheryl, it's time to bring that china out again."

When Rich died, and I somehow survived the pain of it all, I knew I shouldn't limit God's plans for me anymore. That was part of my process of preparation. As I saw how He healed me and worked everything so perfectly together for my good, I realized that with the God I serve, *no dream is too big*. If my goal is to glorify Him, then He will honor my goals. Now, I eat every meal on my fine china. I'm not afraid anymore. I try to be ready for whenever the Lord says, "This is what I want you to do...No, Sheryl. I mean I want you to do it *now*. You don't need to stop and prep. You have been preparing this whole time. So go on...you can do it! I believe in you!"

I had a situation exactly like this happen to me at Encounter 2013, our church's annual women's conference. It was the second night, and I was on the platform singing with the rest of the worship team. Our Women's Pastor, Danielle, had called all the single women to the front of the sanctuary to be prayed over. Then a strange thing happened. She surprisingly said, "I'm going to have Sheryl Beck pray over you." I could tell I was making an odd face, as my brain, ears and eyes argued over the input being received.

Ears: She said *my* name.
Brain: No, that can't be right! I mean, she would have given me a heads up in advance...wouldn't she?
Ears: I should really react, because I'm certain she said *my* name.
Eyes: Umm...people are looking at me.
Brain: Okay, this is a real thing...here we go.

I'm not gonna lie, I was a little freaked out. My prayer was...different. It was more like a three way conversation between me, Jesus and all the women out there. It wasn't your typical prayer, but I felt like Jesus directed every word. I'm more of a planner, so being put on the spot felt uncomfortable to me, but it was a perfect lesson; I am preparing daily for whatever the Lord calls me to do. I can be ready at a moment's notice.

When?
The Later

There is another aspect of the *When* that I want you to consider. Your dreams and purposes you're preparing for (or accomplishing) right now are not the end of the line. They are meant to be stepping stones to the dreams and purposes you will have later; from glory to glory, remember? For example, when I was 17, I joined my first worship team. It was…umm…let's just say a *while* back. I was, and still am in love with worshipping the Lord. Being a part of that team was a goal accomplished, but it wasn't the end. It was training ground for the next goal. I am happy with where I am in regards to my goals right now, but I am not satisfied.

There is more, so much more that this brave soul dares to dream of! Are you being brave with your dreams? Don't get me wrong, you should absolutely be proud of and celebrate what you are currently accomplishing, but you should mix in a little bit of excitement over what's next!

I read a quote by Steven Furtick that forever changed how I looked at myself in regards to my goals and dreams. He said, "If you're not daring to believe God for the impossible, you're sleeping through some of the best parts of your Christian life. And further still: if the size of your vision isn't intimidating to you, there's a good chance it's insulting to God."

Oh – My – Gosh!! In that moment I felt two things: a massive challenge and that I was being given permission to dream extravagant dreams! Oh the freedom! We all know Philippians 4:13 (NLT): "For I can do everything through Christ, who gives me strength."

I usually remind myself of this scripture when my day is going kinda lame or when my teenager is making me a little crazy. I think it has become the Christian's version of The Little Engine That Could and his pep talk to himself. "I think I can. I think I can." But, is that really all it is supposed to be? Have we put that scripture in a box? The same scripture in the Amplified translations says this: "I have strength for all things in Christ Who empowers me [I am ready for anything and equal to anything through Him Who infuses inner strength into me; I am self-sufficient in Christ's sufficiency]."

I love that it says, "I am ready for anything!" All of a sudden I hear the Lord saying to me, "Sheryl, you and I...we're going to soar together." That's the kind of scripture you can read and feel the wind gust through your hair. It can make us energized and invigorated for the future the Lord has planned for us.

You name it; together, the Lord and I can accomplish it! Whatever dream I dream, according to the Word, I am *equal* to it! Whatever dream you dream — according to the Word — you are *equal* to it! So, go ahead - you might as well dream some extraordinary dreams!

Chapter 14:

How?

"Trust Me... I got this!" –God

I want to pretend that the next question comes out calm; in a sing-song voice similar to what a Disney princess would use while wandering through a forest. In a beautiful melody, sing, "How shall I go about this, Lord?" The reality, however, (for me at least) is that it actually comes out sounding a bit more dramatic: "Really, Lord? How in the world am I supposed to do this?!? You have a plan, right? Oh God, tell me, *You* have, a plan!!"

This emphatic outburst comes complete with flailing arms and a swipe of nonexistent sweat from my furrowed brow. I'm not a strategist by nature (or a Disney princess for that matter), so I don't receive the vision and then all of a sudden start setting the plan. I receive the vision, freak out a little, grab my stomach as it experiences pangs of anxiety, then sit back for a second, think on it, and hesitantly say, "Okaaayyy, that sounds good." Kind of like my first date reply to Larry. "I guess that would be alright..."

It's not the neatest process, but it's mine, and while I'm sure the Lord rolls His eyes at me a little bit, it's with love and patience. He knows that after I freak out, I am totally onboard.

Have you ever watched the television show The A-Team? It was on from 1983 to 1987. The show is the epitome of the question *how.* The leader comes up with a grandiose plan, the team all looks at one another, all with skeptical looks on their faces, and right when you think one or all of them is going to say, "No way! That's never going to work!" instead they all declare the do-ability of the plan. (And, yes, I know that "do-ability" isn't really a word.) "Failure-shmailure! We can totally do this!" they say. In my head they said it like that every episode.

It is the same with us and the Lord. We hear a plan, and our faith in His ability and leadership should bring about the "Yes I can!" that He has planted inside of us. Let's recap how the "A-Team" would go about their (always) successful endeavors.

First, they formulated a clever plan. For us, it is God who creates the plan. In Jeremiah 29:11 (MSG), the Lord says, "I know what I'm doing. I have it all planned out—plans to take care of you, not abandon you, plans to give you the future you hope for." *He* is the leader with the plan. You don't need to concern yourself with creating one yourself. He's already got it all under control, and will communicate it to you as you need to know it. Don't get huffy over the fact that He probably isn't going to share the whole big picture with you. Besides, you wouldn't understand the big picture even if He showed it to you, so be content with what He does tell you.

Next, they would discuss the plan so it was clear to everyone involved. Habakkuk 2:2 (NKJV) tells us, "Write the vision and make it plain on tablets, that he may run who reads it." Obviously, the A-Team had read the Bible, because that's exactly what they would do. How about you? Have *you* written down your vision? Is it clear to you and those with whom you share your life? If not, take some time and write it down. As you write it, you may be tempted to tone it down some. Don't! That reaction is based out of fear, but remember, we don't have a spirit of fear, so go ahead – be bold and daring. Write down that dream in all its magnificent splendor!

Then, the A-Team would clarify the roles of each member within the plan. Your part of the plan is simple, yet multi-faceted. You need to seek the Lord. Jeremiah 29:13 (MSG) says, "When you come looking for me, you'll find me. Yes, when you get serious about finding me and want it more than anything else, I'll make sure you won't be disappointed." Be in prayer and in the Word about your purpose. Listen for Him. Don't let the idea of this become a source of anxiety.

In John 10:27 (AMP) He says, "The sheep that are My own hear and are listening to My voice; and I know them, and they follow Me." Trust me, you'll know Him when you hear Him.

After an understanding of the plan was established, then came preparation. The team went into every possible scenario, no matter how crazy or far-fetched, to prepare for success.

We too, should live our lives prepared to succeed! To celebrate our first anniversary, Larry and I planned a trip for a hot and sunny week on the beach in Puerto Vallarta. On the day we left for Mexico, it was 61 degrees in Seattle, but we were dressed in shorts, ready for where we were headed, not for where we were leaving. Dress, speak, think, and live for where God's calling is *taking* you, not for what you are leaving behind!

You are headed for success and victory, so speak, think and live victoriously! This is a crucial part of the preparation that a lot of us overlook. It's called walking in confidence! Haven't attained your goals yet? So what! Have the confident faith that it's only a matter of time.

2 Corinthians 5:7 (NLV) tells us, "Our life is lived by faith. We do

not live by what we see in front of us." Larry and I couldn't feel the Mexican heat while still in Seattle, but we knew we were on our way to sunshine and we were prepared!

Next came implementation of the plan. On the show, things just always seemed to fall into place at the exact right moment. It is the same with the Lord. He will cause all the pieces to fall into place for us. They may not fall comfortably. They may not fall at the moment you or I *think* they should. They may not even be the *pieces* we expected. However, through God's perfection, every piece will fall into place as He has ordained.

The team usually experienced a few bumps in the road. This should come as no surprise, but we will have bumps in the road also. The most important thing to remember is that they never let the setbacks deter them from their goal and neither should we. In John 16:33 (AMP) the Lord gives us both warning and encouragement: "I have told you these things, so that in Me you may have [perfect] peace and confidence. In the world you have tribulation and trials and distress and frustration; but be of good cheer [take courage; be confident, certain, undaunted]! for I have overcome the world. [I have deprived it of power to harm you and have conquered it for you.]" Bumps *will* come. Sometimes they'll slow you down; other times they may knock you over, but just remember to take courage, be confident, certain and undaunted! You are an overcomer!

Finally, as you may have guessed, came success and victory! Now, I can hear what you are thinking, but before you say that's the *A-Team*, of course it worked for *them*. They had writers plotting it all out for them. Let's acknowledge that your entire existence, has been written by God; who just so happens to be the most famous best-selling author...ever! As of April 2013, the Bible had been printed 6,001,500,000 times.

Over two thousand languages have at least a portion of His book! He is the author (and finisher) of our faith. He is the author of salvation, and He is the author of the masterpiece that is your life! You are a part of His team—Team Alpha and Omega—the original A-Team. Maybe you don't hang out with Mr. T., but so what!? All those gold chains would just distract people from how fantastic you are anyway! Here's what's really important:

You are adopted. Ephesians 1:5 (NLT): "God decided in advance to adopt us into his own family by bringing us to himself through Jesus Christ. This is what he wanted to do, and it gave him great pleasure."

You are able. 2 Timothy 3:16, 17 (AMP): "Every Scripture is God-breathed (given by His inspiration) and profitable for instruction, for reproof and conviction of sin, for correction of error and discipline in obedience, [and] for training in righteousness (in holy living, in conformity to God's will in thought, purpose, and action), so that the man of God may be complete and proficient, well fitted and thoroughly equipped for every good work."

You are armed. Ephesians 6:11-17 (NLT): "Put on all of God's armor so that you will be able to stand firm against all strategies of the devil. For we are not fighting against flesh-and-blood enemies, but against evil rulers and authorities of the unseen world, against mighty powers in this dark world, and against evil spirits in the heavenly places. Therefore, put on every piece of God's armor so you will be able to resist the enemy in the time of evil. Then after the battle you will still be standing firm. Stand your ground, putting on the belt of truth and the body armor of God's righteousness. For shoes put on the peace that comes from the Good News so that you will be fully prepared. In addition to all of these, hold up the shield of faith to stop the fiery arrows of the devil. Put on salvation as your helmet, and take the sword of the Spirit, which is the word of God."

You are appointed. John 15:16 (NIV): "You did not choose me, but I chose you and appointed you so that you might go and bear fruit — fruit that will last — and so that whatever you ask in my name the Father will give you."

You are an ambassador. 2 Corinthians 5:20 (TLB): "We are Christ's ambassadors. God is using us to speak to you: we beg you, as though Christ himself were here pleading with you, receive the love he offers you — be reconciled to God."

You are adored. 1 John 4:10 (VOICE): "This is the embodiment of true love: not that we have loved God first, but that He loved us and sent His unique Son on a special mission to become an atoning sacrifice for our sins."

You are an adventurer. 1 Corinthians 1:7-9 (MSG): "Just think — you don't need a thing, you've got it all! All God's gifts are right in front of you as you wait expectantly for our Master Jesus to arrive on the scene for the finale. And not only that, but God himself is right alongside to keep you steady and on track until things are all wrapped up by Jesus. God, who got you started in this spiritual adventure, shares with us the life of his Son and our Master Jesus. He will never give up on you. Never forget that."

You are awesome. Psalms 139:14 (VOICE): "I will offer You my grateful heart, for I am Your unique creation, filled with wonder and awe. You have approached even the smallest details with excellence; Your works are wonderful; I carry this knowledge deep within my soul."

You are all of these things! You're partnered with a God who, according to Ephesians 3:20 (NKJV), "is ABLE to do exceedingly ABUNDANTLY ABOVE ALL that we ask or think, according to the power that works in us." There is no way for you to *not* be successful! Trust me, with the Lord, you *can* do all things. When you fulfill the God-given purpose you're currently working towards, and then prepare to move on to the next big dream, our team leader (the Lord) will give you a wink and say, "I love it when a plan comes together!"

Chapter 15:

Why?

"Eventually you can see that your pain was part of a much larger picture that God was carefully painting."
–James MacDonald

I believe the answer to our last question is the most rewarding. The question is *Why?* And His answer is, "Because this is what I created you for." Ephesians 2:10 (NLT) says, "For we are God's masterpiece. He has created us anew in Christ Jesus, so we can do the good things he planned for us long ago."

We have talked a lot about the Lord bringing all of the pieces together to create something for us, but what we often neglect is the fact that *we* are a piece of something that God is creating for the world; His body the church. 1 Corinthians 12:27 (NLT) clarifies: "All of you together are Christ's body, and each of you is a part of it."

Together we can accomplish immeasurably beyond what we can accomplish as individuals or even sects. It is vitally important that we work together towards the goal of making Jesus famous. Not only to *say* we're working together, but actually doing it. This is the greatest (and often most difficult step) on the way to success. I really think in the *Why* is where we do the most personal growth and development. Here is where we learn to value ourselves and the role we play. In addition to valuing ourselves, we learn to value the people we are aligning ourselves with. This helps us to see the importance and strength of working together, instead of competing and comparing ourselves to one another.

Learning to value ourselves is a sticky wicket for some of us. We have allowed words spoken about us to take root in our hearts, bringing forth bitter fruit. We can spend our entire lives focusing on what others have said or felt about us; even agreeing with them and starting to speak it about ourselves. But to what end? Shame? Pain? A de-valued sense of self? Not a single acceptable option in the bunch! The only thing that will come from this is a life lived with a victim mentality.

While things — traumatic things — have happened to you, through Christ you are an overcomer. So, while it's easy to stay in the rut of thinking about the pain that we have experienced, we need to acknowledge that there is nothing good or healthy for us there. Pain hurts, and continues to hurt unless we escape it. We can make the choice to free ourselves from those thoughts that seek to hold us captive. I understand…it's hard to get out of a rut. The mud wants to suck us down. But the payoff is grand! Your motivation to refresh your thinking about who you are and what you are capable of is monumental; it is possible through God's love for you!

Every negative experience — every harsh word we have heard or thought about ourselves — all pales in comparison to God's adoration for us. God's love for us is so strong that nothing can separate us from it; not death, life, angels, principalities, powers, nothing created now or in the future. That's how powerful His love is for us! He knew every word you would speak, everything you would do before you were even born, and still He loved you. Not only did He love you, but He entrusted you with a purpose. You're afraid? You can push through the fear with the knowledge that He made you specifically for this life and this purpose!

Don't let self-doubt keep you from your mission! Feel ill-equipped? Ask Him for help, but know that you were made for this – literally! Besides, it would take a really prideful person to put more value on their opinion of themselves than the opinion of the Lord. Remember that when you're speaking anything over yourself that is less than *I am fearfully and wonderfully made*!

It is also important to learn the value of partnership. You may be familiar with the story of the Tower of Babel from Genesis 11:1-9. It speaks so powerfully to the strength of a team. Here is the story from the New Living Translation:

"At one time all the people of the world spoke the same language and used the same words. As the people migrated to the east, they found a plain in the land of Babylonia and settled there. They began saying to each other, 'Let's make bricks and harden them with fire.' (In this region bricks were used instead of stone, and tar was used for mortar.) Then they said, 'Come, let's build a great city for ourselves with a tower that reaches into the sky. This will make us famous and keep us from being scattered all over the world.' But the Lord came down to look at the city and the tower the people were building. 'Look!' he said. 'The people are united, and they all speak the same language. After this, nothing they set out to do will be impossible for them! Come, let's go down and confuse the people with different languages. Then they won't be able to understand each other.' In that way, the Lord scattered them all over the world, and they stopped building the city. That is why the city was called Babel, because that is where the Lord confused the people with different languages. In this way he scattered them all over the world."

Sure, this team had a negative plan; the story is about rebellion and pride. But, there is something important we non-prideful, anti-rebellion types can learn from this historical recount. The Lord Himself acknowledged that if the people were united, there was nothing that would be impossible for them. As He is no respecter of persons (Acts 10:34), what was true of those people is also true of us right now.

All of these people had one goal, albeit not a God-approved goal, but one goal: build a tower into the heavens so they wouldn't be scattered across the earth. The scriptures don't divulge their process or state how many people were involved, but I think it's safe to say that everyone played a unique part in the planning and building process. Granted, I've never tried to build a tower into the heavens, but I would imagine my crew wouldn't get much done if we were all assigned the same task of securing the ladders, or if everyone held the position of "Chief Brick Maker." If they were *united* like the Word says they were, then they were more than likely in agreement over the fact that there were *many* roles to be filled; each being important to the overall success of the project.

If we, then, are to be united, let's recognize we each have a special part to play and that our part will be different (yet equally valuable) than the part that our brothers and sisters in Christ play. I sometimes struggle with comparing myself to others, especially other people in the same ministry. I don't compare success vs. success, I seem to compare what *I'm* doing vs. what *they* are doing. Is this good? No. Am I proud of it? Of course not, but no one is perfect, and I am hoping my vulnerability about this weakness and what the Lord has shared with me about it helps you as it has helped me.

Often the Lord will give me dreams to tell me something, and since I had all of those pregnancy dreams before Rich died, I try really hard to pay attention when I feel like I've just had a Jesus dream. Recently, the Lord revealed a lesson to me about comparing myself to others.

In the dream, I was in my backyard looking at the fruit I was growing along the fence. My neighbor, who is someone else on my ministry team, was also growing fruit along their fence. They were growing blueberries, which just so happens to be my favorite fruit. Their blueberry bush was completely full, overflowing with lush, beautiful berries. I looked at the bush *very* longingly and then looked back at my fruit. Mine wasn't a blueberry bush. It was actually an odd amalgamation of three different types of fruit: a pear, a pomegranate and a bunch of blueberries. I had one in my hand. I looked at my fruit in my hand, and then I looked over the fence at the blueberry bush my teammate was growing. While I was focused on the other side of the fence, peering at their fruit, someone took my fruit right out of my hand. I was annoyed that they would take it from me and had a "Hey! That's mine!" kind of reaction, but I quickly realized they wouldn't have been able to steal it from me if I hadn't been focusing all of my attention on the blueberries next door.

The next morning, I thought about the dream over and over, and realized that my fruit, though different, would be delicious to the Lord, but I had to take care of it. It was mine to steward. Was it odd? Yeah, a little bit, but as it turns out, *I'm* a little odd. I like that about myself and so does the Lord. It was a good lesson for me. If we are to be unified, let's appreciate how the Lord uses us differently and not turn this idea into fodder for comparison or competition.

God does things with completion in mind. Even when He created His body (the church) He made us complete. 1 Corinthians 12 speaks at length about how he created the church and why He did it that way. He likens us to a physical body, with eyes, ears and hands. Each part plays a vital role that benefits the whole body. I am meant to walk in *my* purpose alongside others who are walking in *their* purpose. That's the way to be successful, but...have you ever played a "just for fun" game of baseball?

Everyone is given a position; one person goes to first base, another is on second base and so on and so forth. Despite the clear position assignments, there always seems to be that one person who goes after the fly ball *wherever* it is headed on the field. "I got it! I got it!" they say, while running across the field into a position that isn't theirs.

Meanwhile, the outfielder who is actually meant to catch the ball gets run over by the intruder, causing them both to miss the ball. And, now because the intrusive player isn't where he was supposed to be, yep, you guessed it; RBI. Every time this happens, the team groans with annoyance, and rightfully so. In fact, there is even talk of not inviting *that guy* to play next time.

We don't really want to admit it, but this often happens in the body of Christ. We all have a position (our purpose) that the Lord has called us to. For this metaphor, we're going to call our position short stop. However, there are times (we might as well admit it) when a fly ball goes into right field, we look at the right fielder and think "Hmm...I don't know if he's capable." So we run over to "help," and in doing so, screw up the play. This is not the way to win! The way to win is to excel in *our own* area and encourage our teammates along their way to excellence. In the pursuit of

God's purposes on the earth, there is no such thing as a one man show. Instead, we are a full team; a complete body performing different functions to bring about something marvelous…

Now that you understand how important you are and how important everyone else is, it's time to ask yourself this question: "Am I partnering well?

1 Corinthians 3:8 (NLT) says, "The one who plants and the one who waters work together with the same purpose. And both will be rewarded for their own hard work." You know what you should be doing, but are you doing it? Are you staying in your lane, taking care of *your* responsibilities, all the while rocking it like nobody's business? Because as simple as it sounds, that's *your* part. You were created for the lane you are in. I can already hear you thinking that your lane is too narrow and should be expanded. Maybe you think your neighbor's lane is wider or more glamorous than yours. But, has it occurred to you that your lane *is* going somewhere? It is constantly moving towards something new. Your lane's purpose is facilitating your advancement. If you see your lane as narrow, it's because you're looking to your left and right too much and not keeping your eyes fixed straight ahead at the wide open expanse of life and purpose that God has called you to.

Once we fully comprehend the *Why*, we can see how valuable we are in the family of God and all the people around us. You're starting to get it? Well, then adjust your rearview mirror, buckle up and rev your engine baby! Because you've got places to go! Are you ready?

Chapter 16:
The New Normal

"As you move outside of your comfort zone, what was once the unknown and frightening becomes your new normal."
–Robin S. Sharma

I don't want to be trite about this next season you've found yourself in. It's likely that you were completely caught off guard by the changes you've experienced and are still coping. I completely understand! For me, it was encouraging to know that the Lord was working on my behalf and that He was healing me, but even still, I needed time to just be sad; to feel the loss; to mourn.

Sadness and mourning is totally normal and healthy. What isn't healthy is allowing yourself to get *stuck* in your feelings of loss, continuously. Picture me, at the cemetery, ankle deep in the mud. Speaking on behalf of someone who was there, it wasn't a pretty picture. Getting stuck is messy and gross...best to avoid it completely if you can.

Once you're ready for what's next, because there is a *next* available to you, there are some things to consider:

- Don't hold on too tightly to the *was*. Shift your confidence to the *is now* and build faith for the *will be*.

- The transition is a journey, not a destination.

- The Lord is always enhancing, enlarging and increasing. This is not a slight against the life you had which you may have been perfectly content with. What I mean by this is that through this process, God will change YOU for the better.

- The "Yes" is mine to give.

Chapter 17:

The WAS, the IS and the WILL BE

"I'm about to do something brand new." –God (Isaiah 43:19)

When something happens unexpectedly it's hard to view what you lost as a *was*.

Rich and I had been married for over thirteen years. To use the word *was* in the context of our life together was really tough. That made us officially past tense and that was painful. It was a huge loss, and I needed to heal, but I knew a time would come when I would have to let go of the life I had known and have confidence in the *here and now* and faith for the future. This certainly doesn't happen overnight, and if you are in the beginning stages of saying things like, "I was" or "we were," please don't feel like I am trying to rush you. You and the Lord will work out your timing, but eventually you will wake up and your focus won't be on what *was*, but instead you will be able to concentrate on *what is*.

Mathew was a huge motivator for me. Praise God for that boy! I knew I had to get it together for his sake. He was looking to me for cues on how to cope, how to mourn and how to let the Lord heal. That meant taking things one day at a time; a slow process for sure, but we were moving ahead (inching at times, but that was still forward progress). Like driving a car, I would look in the rear view mirror pretty consistently, but for the safety of my family, I couldn't crane my neck and focus solely on what was behind us.

The Bible talks time and again about God moving forward, wanting to do a new thing. He isn't stationary or passive and doesn't want to see those traits in His children either. The Bible doesn't talk about ponds, which are known for their stagnancy, but it does speak often of rivers. John 7:38 (AMP) says, "He who believes in Me [who cleaves to and trusts in and relies on Me] as the Scripture has said, from his innermost being shall flow [continuously] springs and rivers of living water."

We've already touched on the differences between ponds and rivers, but I'd like to reiterate. Ponds are known for their calm stillness; they don't feed into other bodies of water. A pond is calm and picturesque from the outside, but under the water's surface it's really messy.

Rivers, on the other hand, are constantly moving, sometimes tumultuously. They often align themselves with other rivers, joining forces along the way. Their water is often more clear. Rivers are continually changing their environment. You are most likely seeing pros and cons for both ponds and rivers, but the question of the day is this: "Which does God want *you* to be?" Hint: See John 7:38.

He wants you to be aligning yourself with other believers, instead of standing stoically alone. He wants you to have clarity instead of a murky outlook on your life. He desires you to be moving from what *was* into *what is*, and like a river, your movement changes your environment. I know rivers can be scarier than ponds, but rivers get things done. Tumultuous moments will come, but the Lord will help you to find your new footing.

Accepting where you are right now is the key that ultimately unlocks the door to your future. The present — the *is* — is what we most take for granted, but it's the one timeframe we can actually enjoy. We are learning from our past and preparing for our future, but the present — the *right now* — this is where it's at people! Don't waste today and its events by longing for how it was before or even how you hope it will be someday. Your present and new normal is the foundation for what will be. Get the most out of *now*.

Your contributions to the foundation will have a huge impact on its strength and ability to secure your future. What are you folding into the mixture? Are you adding in fear, or faith? Are you tossing in some anxiety, or peace? Hold the phone…did you just throw in some hopelessness?! Well you'd better pull that back out real quick before it gets cemented in.

We've been given instructions on what to mix into our foundation and here they are: "Finally, brothers and sisters, whatever is true, whatever is noble, whatever is right, whatever is pure, whatever is lovely, whatever is admirable — if anything is excellent or praiseworthy — think about such things." Philippians 4:8 (NIV)

I was surprised to find that once I decided to embrace my present, to make the most of each day, and to enjoy what the Lord brought me within it, all of a sudden, the future I was hoping and preparing for started showing itself. I realized that making the most of every day was actually part of the preparation for my future. I was walking in faith for the *will be*.

The Lord has an understanding of the entire picture from the *was* to the *will be* long before we get there. Deuteronomy 31:8 (NIV) tells us, "The Lord himself goes before you and will be with you; he will never leave you nor forsake you. Do not be afraid; do not be discouraged." The process may be painful, but the pain is purposeful: they are growing pains. Your spiritual muscles are being built stronger so you can be better equipped to handle your future.

The new can seem daunting, but just remember He has been preparing you. He has made you into a new wine skin so you can hold the fresh wine; the fresh anointing for your new season. Matthew 9:17 (NLT) says, "And no one puts new wine into old wineskins. For the old skins would burst from the pressure, spilling the wine and ruining the skins. New wine is stored in new wineskins so that both are preserved." And Mark 2:22 (TLB) tells us, "You know better than to put new wine into old wineskins. They would burst. The wine would be spilled out and the wineskins ruined. New wine needs fresh wineskins."

The plans God has for you are extraordinary and require a new you. Your *was* may have been really good. You may have been perfectly content with your life — I know I was — but this is what I learned: my life as it was didn't have the capacity to contain the great of my *will be*. It is the same for you.

I know letting go is painful, and I am truly sorry for that. But, as difficult as it may be to move on, maintaining a tight grip on the past keeps you from experiencing all the new that God has planned. I think Marilyn Monroe summed it up best when she said, "…sometimes good things fall apart so better things can fall together."

Chapter 18:

The Transition

Switchbacks and bee stings and Starbucks... oh my!

The transition from one season into the next is usually pretty yucky. There's no point in sugar coating it...you and I both know it's the truth. I liken transition to hiking to a beautiful destination. In fairness, I should throw out the disclaimer that I'm not really an outdoor kinda girl, and hiking is LOW on my "let's do this" list! But anyway, step one is driving to the location from where the hike will begin. Ahhhh....the car is air conditioned, the radio is playing all your favorite songs. It's a comfy drive; all is well. You arrive at the trailhead, and get out of the car. Yowza! It's hot out here!

The atmosphere in which you've found yourself is really different than what you're used to. It's a bit of a shock, but you have confidence it's all going to be fine. You ask your Guide how long the trek will be, but He can't really give you a definitive answer. All He says is, "Ultimately, it's up to you." His answer isn't exactly what you had hoped, but you are convinced that the beautiful scene at the end will make it all worthwhile. Besides, you have everything you need; water, snacks, good hiking attire, and shoes, and reliable hiking companions. There is no map, per se, but you do have your Guide, so you're feeling good. Off you go.

In the beginning stage of the hike, your body is still getting acclimated to the heat and physical exertion. You aren't normally a hiker, but this time is special so you suck it up and decide to be a trooper. You drink your water consistently and rest when you need to. Your traveling companions are sticking close and your Guide is leading the way, so you feel secure. All of a sudden, you see a meadow of wild flowers and, "Oh, look!" there's a family of deer. You really want to go see the nice deer family, but it's not on the path. The Guide says, "Yes, that is nice, but trust Me, where we are headed... is beyond amazing." But, you want to see the deer closer, so you decide to check them out anyway.

The Guide is perplexed at your choice. He knows what's up ahead. He's seen it already and knows this scene, though nice, pales in comparison to where He's leading. He knows you are wasting your time, but He is patient nonetheless. He doesn't want you to get lost, so the group halts, waiting for you.

You walk gently through the meadow to get up closer to the deer. You quickly realize, that sometimes, what is picturesque from a distance, is actually much different up close. You just stepped in mushy deer droppings and the wild flowers have drawn swarms of bees. The bees have made it clear they don't like you. You recognize that you've made a mistake and head quickly back to the path. You return a little injured and a bit smelly, but it's fine. You've only lost a few minutes. The Guide takes you to a stream to clean you up and tend to your bee stings. "You okay now?" He asks. "Are you ready to move on?" You're a little embarrassed, but He is so kind. You nod a meek *yes*, and with that, your group moves on.

Soon, it's time for lunch. You all sit down near a small pond to rest and eat. You pull the snacks you brought from your bag. Turns out your candy bar and a bottled Starbucks coffee weren't exactly the right choice for a strenuous hike. It's fine...the Guide has brought exactly what you need. He knew this was out of your comfort zone, so He came prepared.

With lunch complete, you start to feel tired. "You know, it's nice here." You say, "Why don't we just spend the rest of the day here?" You've thrown the option out there to the group, but by now everyone has accepted the Guide's expertise as the compass of the trek, so they all look to Him for His input. He looks at you, and you see expectation in His eyes, but He is patient with your request. He is able to see past your words and understand the motive behind them. He comes over, sits next to you and says, "I know you're getting tired. The difficulty of this hike has been more than you anticipated and that's totally fine. We can stop here if that's what you really want, but before you decide, you need to know that by stopping you will be missing out on the entire purpose of this hike. Sure, you will have had a good day. You'll have a story to tell and some pictures to show, but this, here — this pond — this isn't really where you want to be. Deep down, you know you want to go all the way. I'm going to be honest with you. You might struggle here and there along the rest of the path, but I will be right next to you. If it gets to be too much, I will carry you. Please believe me when I say that it will all be worth it in the end. Will you trust me in this and keep moving?"

You think on that for a moment and decide two things:
1. Yes, you will trust the Guide, and
2. Yes, you really do want to go all the way!

Finally after what feels like *forever*, you round a bend, reaching the end of the hike. You are completely astounded at what you see. It is completely glorious! More beautiful than you *ever* imagined. Your Guide is standing next to you, and He is an amalgamation of several emotions. First, He is so proud of you and the journey you endured. Second, He is grateful to your traveling companions for journeying with you. Lastly, He is excited. He is excited *for* you to be where you are. It is truly a spectacle of everything you've always loved and so many things you never ever thought you'd have the opportunity to experience. You are so happy! The bee stings still ache a little; a reminder that you should have just listened to the Guide, but you are here. You made it!

That hike my friend, is the transition. It can be a mix of switchbacks, bee stings and alluring distractions, but with the proper traveling companions and the Guide who sees the big picture, you will make it through to something that will dazzle and delight!

There will most likely be painful aspects of the transition journey. For me, the switchbacks were memories that would spring up at inconvenient times. The bee stings were birthdays and holidays that should have been spent together. Coping with those memories and days were part of the course I was enduring.

Galatians 6:9 (NLV) instructs us, "Do not let yourselves get tired of doing good. If we do not give up, we will get what is coming to us at the right time."

I'm not going to even pretend that the hiker I mentioned wasn't me. On my hike, I asked the Guide questions like, "Why are we going this way? The other way seems better." I got distracted by pretty, flower-filled meadows and peaceful looking deer, who took one look at me and charged. I found myself near cool ponds and wanted to set up a permanent camp there, but I trusted the Guide and really did want to go all the way. I felt like Frank Sinatra about the whole thing: "If I can make it there, I'll make it anywhere..." So, I choose every day to keep going. I know what the Lord has for me is beyond my expectations. We can be encouraged in this by the Word.

Ecclesiastes 7:8 (NLV): "The end of something is better than its beginning. Not giving up in spirit is better than being proud in spirit." Your Guide on this hike is saying, "Don't give up – at the end is something better." So, grab your water, and let's get a move on!

Chapter 19:

Our God the Upgrader!

"... who by His mighty power at work within us is able to do far more than we would ever dare to ask or even dream of..."
–Ephesians 3:20

Maya Angelou, a woman who experienced both emotional and physical trauma, once said, "I can be changed by what happens to me. But, I refuse to be reduced by it." I feel the same way. The God I serve is not a God of subtraction - His math somehow always equals more. I don't care how it looks going into the math equation, with God the outcome will always be more than you expected. It looks like this:

Everything < God!

Now that's the kind of math I can get behind! Geometry and calculus…not so much.

History — our own, that of our friends and family, and that which is chronicled in the Bible — has shown pretty consistently that when God makes a change, especially a significant change, it is ultimately a change for the better. In the midst of hardship, however, we often make a habit of aligning ourselves *with* our difficulties. In so doing, we label ourselves, and usually the moniker leans towards the negative.

Even so, like with everything else in life, we have a choice in this. The easy route is to claim the name *Victim*, and the reality may be that you *have* been a victim. But, you don't have to let it define you.

You have survived, and in that survival you have earned a new name. You can now call yourself *Victorious*. I wore the badge of *Widow* until I decided to trade it in for one that said *Wonder Woman*.

It may sound silly, but Wonder Woman is the goal I've always set for myself. I grew up with her, intrigued by her choice and ability to redefine herself. No, I don't have a golden lasso or an invisible plane (although that would be cool), but you know what I do have? I have a loving Father who says I am fearfully and WONDERfully made! And, like Wonder Woman, I choose to be brave and courageous, knowing that with Jesus I can do all things! The example of declaring powerful words over ourselves is set for us in Joel 3:10b (MSG). "Let the weak one throw out his chest and say, 'I'm tough, I'm a fighter.' Go ahead – say it aloud: "I am tough! I am a fighter!" Declare a new name for yourself!

Need some suggestions? How about Champion, Overcomer, or Warrior? If you're a woman, I would even be happy to *share* the title of "Wonder Woman" with you, because with Jesus you are all of these things!

In the Bible, there are examples of God actually changing people's names in preparation for their new and blessed season. Let's talk about two: Abram and Jacob.

Abram became Abraham in Genesis 17:4-6 (VOICE). "Here is My covenant with you. I promise you will become the root of a huge family tree of multiple nations. To symbolize your foundational role in this covenant, I hereby change your name. You will no longer go by the name 'Abram.' Your new name will be 'Abraham,' which means 'father of a great multitude of nations,' because that is exactly what I will make of you. Your descendants will be exceedingly fruitful. Nations and kings will descend from you."

His original name (Abram) was good on its own. It meant "High Father" or "Exalted Father." No complaints there, right? But, his new name was "Abraham, meaning father of a great multitude of nations, wasn't just a cool adjective and a noun. There seemed to be a built-in purpose in it, declaring his new present and future. Where "High Father" says this is who you are now, "father of a great multitude of nations" says this is what I have for your destiny and what the world, itself, will gain from you. With this new name came unlimited possibilities!

Jacob was given the new name of "Israel" in Genesis chapter 32 (AMP). "[The Man] asked him, 'What is your name?' And [in shock of realization, whispering] he said, 'Jacob' supplanter, schemer, trickster, swindler! And He said, 'Your name shall be called no more Jacob [supplanter], but Israel [contender with God]; for you have contended and have power with God and with men and have prevailed.'"

This conversation took place between Jacob and "a Man": the Lord. This is clarified for us in Genesis 35:9-10 (AMP), where it explains, "And God [in a distinctly visible manifestation] appeared to Jacob again when he came out of Padan-aram, and declared a blessing on him. Again God said to him, 'Your name is Jacob [supplanter]; you shall not be called Jacob any longer, but Israel shall be your name.' So He called him Israel [contender with God]."

Awesome – Jacob went from a swindler to a contender! (Is anyone else hearing Marlon Brando from On the Waterfront in their heads? "I coulda been a contender!") Talk about an upgrade! Like with Abraham, his new name given by the Lord also had future implications. He said, "You…have power with God and with men." It wasn't for just that moment. The power was given in his present to be used for his future and the future of many! His lineage became known as the Twelve Tribes of Israel, and from one of these tribes — the tribe of Judah — came Jesus the Messiah.

Both of these men had a process they went through to become the men God called them to be. Abraham waited…and waited. Israel, wrestled, and wouldn't let go.

Your current season is part of your process. Through it, be confident that you're becoming who God called you to be.

I'd like to tell you about an interesting conversation the Lord and I had about my process.

It was a beautiful day. Larry and I were driving around in his little convertible Porsche, and I remember feeling so odd; that my life was now so immensely different than what it had been. I asked the Lord, "Why did you not heal Rich, because I know that you could have?" As ridiculous as this may sound, there was no emotion involved; no anger or sadness. It was a question born solely out of curiosity. I know the truth is He *could have* healed him. He could have even raised him from the dead if He wanted to, but He chose not to. I just really wanted to know why. Truthfully, I didn't *need* to know why. I just *wanted* to. There is a huge difference! Good Fathers make sure that their kids have everything they need, but not always everything they want, and that's okay. I may never know the *Why* until Heaven, but there are some things that I do know.

I know that losing Rich was always meant to be a part of my story. I know that losing him provided me an opportunity to lean on the Lord more so than I had ever done before. I know that despite pain, I can be a victorious child of the Most High God. I know, not think, but *know* God used my most difficult season to upgrade ME! He used the loss to prepare me for what was next. None of it was in vain. It prepared me for all that I have now; this amazing life where I am daring and brave and trying to live a limitless "outside of my comfort zone" life for Jesus; a future full of successes that point back to Him. I've grown so much in my relationship with God that I have become the Wonder Woman I was always meant to be.

Chapter 20:

Saying Yes

"I am willing to do whatever he wants." –Mary (Luke 1:38)

If you want anything in life, anything at all, it all begins by saying "Yes." Yes I can do it. Yes I will try. Yes I will take a chance. It is the scariest word in the English language, but it is also the bravest, most courage-laden word that has ever been spoken.

The word *yes* opens doors. Walt Disney spoke wisdom in regards to this subject through the movie character Mary Poppins. She said, "Open different doors. You may find a *you* there that you never knew was yours. Anything can happen." By saying *yes*, you will realize that anything can happen...Your *yes* can change the world!

There are so many examples of Yes-Men and Women who've leaned into obedience and made an indelible mark on the world. To name a few: Noah, Mary and Isaiah.

God is in the habit of asking things that seem, well, strange. I was going to say ridiculous, but that seemed a little sacrilegious. Let's look at Noah's *yes* for a second. I'm going to paraphrase...

The human race made God sorry He'd ever created them, so he wanted to wipe 'em out and start from scratch with Noah. Noah was a keeper. God had confidence in Noah and felt good about their relationship, so God went to Noah with His plan.

God: "Noah, the Earth and the people who cover it...I'm over it!

This is what we're going to do. You are going to make a boat. I'll give you the plans. I'll give you the resources. After the boat is built, I'm going to flood this whole place, wiping out everyone and everything. You and I are good, so we're going to have a covenant between you and I that will secure your life and that of your family. I know what you're thinking: nothing like this has ever happened before. I get it. You are a little overwhelmed, but you can trust me. Are we on the same page? Can I count on you?"

Then, in Genesis 6:22 (VOICE) came Noah's response, "So Noah listened to God, and he built the ark. He did everything God asked him to do." That was a resounding *yes*, and I for one am very thankful! One rocky boat ride and thousands of years later this *yes* is still acknowledged as a huge moment in history.

With Noah, the request was ridiculous…oops, I mean strange. With Mary, well, the word *impossible* comes to mind. Bring a baby into the world through a virgin mother? Okay. Sure. Totally. Oh, wait, that doesn't sound right, but with God ALL things are possible. The angel, Gabriel, brought the news to the mom-to-be. Again, paraphrasing…

Gabriel: "Good morning Mary! Oh, I'm sorry. I didn't mean to startle you, but I just wanted to bring you an important message from the Lord. You are going become pregnant and have a son. He will be the son of the Most High. We can all agree that this plan raises some valid questions, but the Holy Spirit will take care of all of that. Are you with me?"

In Luke 1:38 (MSG), we see the amazing faith that drew the Lord's attention to Mary in the first place: "And Mary said, 'Yes, I see it all now: I'm the Lord's maid, ready to serve. Let it be with me just as you say.'" She came on board with God's vision and without hesitation claimed that vision as her own!

Noah embraced the strange, Mary saw possible in the impossible and Isaiah, well, he just wanted to serve. In Isaiah 6:8 (NIV) he says, "Then I heard the voice of the Lord saying, 'Whom shall I send? And who will go for us?' And I said, 'Here am I. Send me!'"

God had a task and Isaiah was just the man for the job. What qualified him? His *yes*. That's what he had going for him. He basically said, "Lord, whatever you need, I'm your guy!"

All three of these yes-men and women were *all in*; eager to be on God's team. You may be asking yourself, "How could they make such a solid commitment just like that!?" (Imagine the finger snap here)

Well, in answer to your question, they understood a couple things about God. First, they knew that He cared about the well-being of His kids. He is the One who sets the best fatherly example of loving and providing for His children. He positions His kids for success.

Secondly, they understood that a *yes* to God equals partnership. "Yes" doesn't mean I will do it on my own. Yes means, "I will partner with You, God, knowing You will do the heavy lifting."

We've talked about only three people who trusted God with their yeses (and ultimately with their lives), but there are *so many* more! Moses, Joseph, Daniel, John the Baptist, the disciples, Paul, my pastor, your pastor…the list goes on and on. Often, we ask God, "Why him and not me?" or we wonder to ourselves, "Why does God use that person and not me?"

Here is the answer we run smack dab into for that question. The main reason is because the people that the Lord consistently uses are like Mary, saying, "Yes, I see it now, and I'm ready to serve." You can be the next yes-man or yes-woman who utilizes that simple and frightening word to change everything. So what's *your* answer?

Chapter 21:

Our Messy Message

"Hardships often prepare ordinary people for an extraordinary destiny." –C.S. Lewis

It is always God's intention to heal us from the pain we experience through loss or struggle. In fact, sometimes, dare I say, usually, a struggle is meant to be the launching pad towards the awesome future that the Lord has for us. Have you ever heard the phrase "He can turn your mess into a message and your test into a testimony?" Let me tell you something – it's true!

My favorite example of this is Joseph. Joseph recognized God's hand in his life and articulated it perfectly while talking to his brothers upon their reunion.

The story begins in Genesis 37. It makes for some good reading…it has adventure, scandal, intrigue, a hero, and more. The story of Joseph is the whole package!

Joseph had rubbed his brothers the wrong way for the last time! They were fed up with his dreams about how *he* was basically better than them. They had finally had it with the mouthy kid, and in their anger, devised a plan to rid themselves of their troublesome sibling. To make a long story, short; they sold him into slavery, and it was a roller coaster ride for Joseph from then on. It was a *mess* and a *test*, but God used the whole situation for good.

There were multiple bumps in the road for Joseph. They came in the form of unfounded accusations, prison time and being (not just feeling) forgotten. At the end of all the heartache, he is reunited with his brothers. Their reunion is described in Genesis 50. In verse 20 (NKJV), Joseph is able to see past the mess, beyond the test and set his eyes upon the purposes that they served. "But as for you, you meant evil against me; but God meant it for good, in order to bring it about as it is this day, to save many people alive."

Notice he doesn't gloss over the fact that what happened to him was horrible, but it also isn't his focus. He is healed, and through his emotional, spiritual and physical health, he clearly sees how the Lord worked it all out for good – not just his good, but for the good of the entire nation.

I know that in this moment, seeing that the Lord has plans for your pain might look hazy. But, regardless of whether or not you see the fruit of it right now, tap into the faith that you have – even if it is just that of a mustard seed – trusting that you *will*.

In the future, you will see how the Lord was working everything – including this painful season – into the big picture: your courageous and victorious life. Maya Angelou has another wise quote I love: "You may encounter many defeats, but you must not be defeated. In fact, it may be necessary to encounter the defeats, so you can know who you are, what you can rise from, how you can still come out of it."

I believe each of us has a measure of bravery, courage, and fearlessness inside us. Unfortunately, many will never make the choice to tap into that potential. Some of us will let it all lay dormant until that critical moment when we need it. That's the category I was in. I'm not proud of it, but it's the truth. I was content to limit myself to being "Rich's wife," constantly down-playing who *I* could be for the Lord.

I didn't even acknowledge the bravery, courage and fearlessness the Lord had planted in me until I absolutely needed it. I allowed fear to become complacency, but the Lord made it clear to me that He had already supplied me with what I needed. If I was going to make it through the *stress of the loss* into the *promise of the future*, it was time to access *all* He had given to me.

Now's the time for you to dig deep. You need all the Lord has planted in you so you can stand tall when you feel like shrinking back.

Our core values come to the surface in times of distress. I believe that relying on the Lord is one of your core values; that's why you've even bothered to get this far in a book about letting the Lord heal you. At some point, you'll be ready to make hard choices you never thought you'd have to make. Allow your reliance on the Lord to be your guide. Remember that His Presence is vital in good seasons as well as rough ones. Seek Godly counsel, encouragement and honest opinions (which may not always be your favorite) from your peeps. And, always keep God's call and purpose for your life in mind.

Allow your faith (that has grown into dependence) be the thing that guides every decision you make from this point forward. Say, "I am weak, but my Father is strong. He will see me through. My circumstance is lame and at times overwhelming, but I make a daily decision to give it all to the Lord. I'm *all in* with however He wants to heal me, and however He wants to grow me."

The Lord will see your commitment to aligning yourself with

Him, and He will absolutely show Himself faithful, leading your healing process. 2 Chronicles 16:9 (NLT) says, "The eyes of the Lord search the whole earth in order to strengthen those whose hearts are fully committed to him." He is constantly on the lookout. Your commitment to Him becomes a spotlight that shines directly on your life and needs. Living a life fully committed to the Lord draws His eye, and He blesses you with every good thing you need to grow in strength.

And then, an amazing day will come...You will meet a person who needs to hear your story.

Don't be afraid to tell them. If you are emotional about it, that's completely fine. The first time (yes it will happen more than once) might be like that, but don't see your emotions as a roadblock. Your emotions will benefit a story that's told genuinely and honestly. Usually "genuine honesty" comes laced with emotion.

This person will be hurting and looking for hope, and they will find it in your testimony. Your experience will resonate with their heart, and you will be able to speak life and encouragement to them. Because you came through, they will believe they can as well.

When that day comes, you will realize that the Lord has redeemed your loss and is using it for your good and for the good of many people around you. As you talk with them about how the Lord brought you through your darkest times and showed you His limitless love, they will be encouraged that He will do the same for them. Though it may not feel like it in this moment, believe me, someday you will tell someone else, "I was bruised, but not broken!"

I couldn't have said it better myself!

About the Author

Sheryl Beck Nelson is a dynamic worship leader and songwriter at her home church; Capital Christian Center in Olympia, Washington, where she attends and serves with her husband Larry and son Mathew. Because of her passionate drive to inspire, she is also a mentor and small group leader investing in the growth and development of all generations of God's daughters. To date, Sheryl has used her story to influence thousands, and because she knows God never wastes a difficult season, she hopes it will also begin the process of healing for you.

www.sherylbecknelson.com

Bruised but Not Broken is proudly published by:

Creative Force Press

www.CreativeForcePress.com

Do You Have a Book in You?